STRATEGIC
FOREIGN
ASSISTANCE

Advance praise for *Strategic Foreign Assistance*

"This book will appeal to all people who are concerned with foreign policy and foreign aid strategies regardless of party. Seeking to strengthen the role of civil society organizations is not a left or right proposition but a thoughtful and practical approach to development and security."

> William P. Fuller, former president of the Asia Foundation

"This excellent book offers innovative ideas for engaging and supporting civil society and enabling it to play a leading role in promoting social and political reform and economic development in the future."

> Radwan A. Masmoudi, president, Center for the Study of Islam & Democracy, Washington, D.C.

"*Strategic Foreign Assistance* is the most encouraging integration of development strategy and civil society building within a two-track diplomacy framework that I have ever seen."

> Joseph V. Montville, diplomat in residence, Center for Global Peace, American University

"This thoughtful book suggests a strategy for success in helping civil society organizations address critical problems in regions where the American government is mistrusted."

> Joseph S. Nye Jr. is distinguished service professor at Harvard and author of *Soft Power: The Means to Success in World Politics*.

STRATEGIC FOREIGN ASSISTANCE

Civil Society in International Security

A. Lawrence Chickering

Isobel Coleman

P. Edward Haley

Emily Vargas-Baron

HOOVER INSTITUTION PRESS
Stanford University   Stanford, California

www.hoover.org

Hoover Institution Press Publication No. 544

First printing, 2006
12 11 10 09 08 07 06   9 8 7 6 5 4 3 2 1

Manufactured in the United States of America

The paper used in this publication meets the minimum requirements
of the American National Standard for Information Sciences—
Permanence of Paper for Printed Library Materials, ANSI Z39.48-1992. ∞

Library of Congress Cataloging-in-Publication Data
Strategic foreign assistance : civil society in international security / by
A. Lawrence Chickering . . . [et al.].
        p.   cm. — (Hoover Institution Press publication ; 544)
    Includes bibliographical references and index.
    ISBN 0-8179-4712-4 (alk. paper)
    1. Terrorism—Prevention—International cooperation. 2. Security,
International. 3. Civil society—Developing countries. 4. Terrorism—
Prevention—Government policy—United States. I. Title: Strategic foreign
assistance. II. Chickering, A. Lawrence. III. Series.
HV6431.S7475 2006
363.325'1525—dc22   2005034967

Contents

Preface

I started thinking about the issues explored in this book in the mid-1980s, a time when non-state actors were starting to play an increasing role in international affairs. At that time I also began to work on economic policy reform in developing countries, and I began to see the powerful roles that local civil society organizations (CSOs) could play in promoting change in countries that resisted advice from other states and from international organizations.

The potential roles of civil society have greatly increased since non-state actors (terrorists) became the principal threats to national and international security. Since 9/11, policymakers have come to feel a greatly increased sense of urgency about promoting democracy, development, and social justice in states that shelter terrorists. In the initiative to promote democracy, serious problems have arisen in a number of countries—most obviously in Iraq. Many of these problems are a consequence of the limited options available to traditional, formal statecraft. Local CSOs need to play a much larger role in promoting changes that cannot be imposed from outside but must come from within.

Over more than a decade, ongoing conversation with William P. Fuller, beginning when he was president of the Asia Foundation, provided an important foundation for understanding a broad range of both theoretical and practical issues on how

CSOs—again, indigenous CSOs—can promote different kinds of change.

In January 2003, the Pacific Council for International Policy sponsored a one-day meeting at the Asia Foundation in San Francisco to explore a wide range of issues related to the role of CSOs in promoting economic, social, and political change. This meeting, which I organized, allowed others to join the conversation, especially focusing on particular issues and reform models. I recruited some of them as coauthors of this book and others made contributions in other ways.

The subject of models and strategies for reform on a wide range of issues is so large that when I started talking to the Hoover Institution about a possible book on the subject, it was clear I needed collaborators—people who specialize in particular issues and someone whose field is general issues of foreign policy and international relations.

The importance of educating girls and empowering women led me to Isobel Coleman, recruited by the Council on Foreign Relations to look at women in developing countries. I also knew that Isobel had worked on institutional problems in USAID that make it difficult to achieve strategic objectives. Emily Vargas-Baron brought an understanding of three important areas: a general understanding of the roles of civil society in solving economic and political problems, special challenges of working in nations both during and after conflicts, and a practical understanding of institutions resulting from her years working in USAID. Edward Haley brought a broad perspective of foreign policy and international relations, with special knowledge of the Middle East, where continuing conflict remains a preoccupying concern of our foreign and national security policies.

A. Lawrence Chickering
San Francisco, California
November 2005

Acknowledgments

A day-long seminar at Claremont-McKenna College in November 2004 provided clarification on a variety of issues important to this book. In addition to the authors, Bill Ascher, Alex Benard, Bill Fuller, and Shamil Idriss attended this seminar, and we wish to thank them for their special contributions. We are also grateful to Claremont-McKenna College for hosting the seminar.

Other contributors in relation both to individual chapters and to the entire book include Shane Adler, Nicolas Ardito-Barletta, Lee Benham, Stephen P. Cohen, Hernando de Soto, Robert B. Hawkins Jr., Marco Konings, John Marks, Alberto Pasco-font, and Harry Rowen. We want to acknowledge and thank them as well.

Finally, we want give special thanks to John Raisian, director of the Hoover Institution, for his commitment to the project and continuing support; to Richard Sousa and Jeff Bliss, also of Hoover, for providing multiple, continuing forms of support ensuring a successful project; and to Andrew Jones, who edited the manuscript.

1. Toward Strategic Foreign Assistance

The attacks of 9/11 showed that some of the most important threats to national security no longer come from a small number of powerful, hostile states but from multitudes of unknown, invisible non-state actors (terrorists), who seek refuge in failed, weak and/or fragile societies. National and international security, therefore, partly depends on engaging failed and weak societies, and encouraging economic, political, legal, and social change within them.

Since the threat has changed, the means necessary to meet the threat must change as well. While the state instruments that protected national security and fostered development for the past half-century remain important for a variety of purposes, they have limited capacity to promote many kinds of desirable changes inside other countries. This is especially true where institutions are weak and the need to promote development of societies is strong.

In this chapter we argue that since some non-state actors are now among the greatest threats to security, foreign policymakers must work with other non-state actors—civil society organizations (CSOs)—to meet the economic, political, and social challenges that underlie these new security threats. To do this, the United States must develop a strategic foreign cooperation and assistance policy that fosters strong civil societies as an important end for promoting development, in addition to its traditional role as a means to deliver aid. This increased focus on civil society should deepen connections with citizens in the failed, weak and/or fragile states that harbor terrorists, and it will identify many citizens of other countries who will work with us because it is in their own and their nation's interest to do so. (It has recently become obvious that advanced democracies like England and France are also breeding terrorists, and we believe increasing emphasis on civil society can help there too. However, our focus here is on developing countries.)

Civil society has an especially important role to play in promoting democracy. The social foundation of democracy is built on political consensus and social trust. The challenges of moving through difficult ventures in relationship-building—whether in bringing Sunnis into the political process in Iraq or in opening the Egyptian political system so the secular democratic groups and the Muslim Brotherhood can play an open role or in encouraging opposition groups like Hamas in Palestine to give up violence—are especially great if the path is bounded by *formal* processes that constrain most government action. Civil society, on the other hand, is uniquely positioned to facilitate *informal* engagement and networking to build relationships of trust to solve these problems and many others.

Building civil society has not been a high priority of U.S. development assistance policy planning. In practice, however, USAID missions have implemented many of their programs through international CSOs, which in turn typically work through local CSO partners. Local civil society organizations, as a result, have burgeoned in the past two decades, undertaking a wide variety of economic, legal, social, and political activities.[1]

1. CSOs are involved in legal reform initiatives, legal aid, environmental research and advocacy, moderate Islamic associations, business and labor as-

In some countries they have promoted significant, positive changes that have been aligned with U.S. foreign policy objectives.[2]

Despite the breadth of CSO activity and influence in many countries, we believe the U.S. foreign policy community and, above all, senior foreign policymakers, should recognize the potential that CSOs have to help achieve U.S. foreign policy objectives.[3] Currently, CSOs do not figure substantially in the larger academic and policymaking debate on international relations and foreign policy.[4] The major reason is a lack of clarity about the strategic roles of civil society and a limited understanding of what is possible. In addition, because of their limited interest in the issue, foreign policymakers tend to regard policy in this area as involving development alone and leave it, therefore, largely to USAID. Although USAID could have a vital role in implementing a new approach, it lacks the political and bureaucratic clout to win approval of investments on a scale capable of accomplishing the strategic objectives at issue. Secretary of State Condoleeza Rice, in recent statements emphasizing the importance of civil society, has indicated a keen awareness of the

---

sociations, public health, educational associations, conflict resolution, sports, community organizations, religious groups, and on and on.

2. These include education for girls (in many countries), institutional, judicial and legal reform (in Pakistan), micro-finance programs (in Bangladesh), voter surveys and education (in Afghanistan and Indonesia), "peoples' assemblies" as quasi-constitutional conventions (in Pakistan), and many others.

3. Although CSOs play almost no role either in policy planning or in the deliberations of the foreign policy community at the working levels of the State Department, ambassadors and embassies maintain much closer contact and cooperation with CSOs than the larger debate would suggest.

4. One can read a year of issues of leading foreign policy journals—*Foreign Affairs, Foreign Policy, The National Interest, Orbis*—without seeing a single, positive article on civil society. Nor can one find discussion of its potential uses in these and other journals on any major foreign policy challenge: in the Middle East, in South Asia, in Sub-Saharan Africa—anywhere.

issue—suggesting a major commitment to change past policy.[5] However, real change is difficult to achieve.[6] As a result, CSOs are not yet playing the role they could in mitigating the conditions that promote terrorism, and in achieving sustainable development.

Building prosperous, developed civil societies can be one of the most powerful antidotes to terrorism. The shift in focus to societies that breed terrorists would follow a long-standing pattern in American development assistance of using foreign aid for strategic purposes. After World War II nearly all U.S. foreign aid went to Western Europe to foster the psychological, political, and economic resources to resist Soviet subversion and aggression. In the late 1950s, U.S. aid shifted to Southeast Asia. In the 1960s, the Alliance for Progress aimed to promote democracy and socio-economic development and meet the Cuban expansionist movement in Latin America. Then in the 1970s

5. Secretary Rice, interview by Jim Lehrer, *Newshour with Jim Lehrer*, PBS, March 4, 2005.

6. A good example of the discrepancy between policymakers' emphasis on civil society and the government's implementation of a new policy is USAID's Fragile States Strategy, which was published in December 2004. The Strategy focuses almost entirely on repairing fragile *states* and barely mentions the separate challenge of reforming societies in fragile states. Its central concern is with "governance," but it is clear that this word refers only to states and governments and not to non-state institutions. This emphasis on states leads naturally to the conclusion that it is impossible to work in some states. Thus, "Not all fragile states provide opportunities for constructive USAID engagement. . . . Outsiders [meaning USAID] are far better equipped to address effectiveness deficits than promote legitimacy." This is only true, as in the case of the Strategy, if one focuses entirely on states and has no strategy for civil society. Outsiders *can* support civil society, with enormous implications for promoting legitimacy of governance understood not only of civil society but even (to some degree and in some instances) of governments.

USAID's Conflict Management and Mitigation Program provides another example of a major, important USAID initiative that professes commitment to communicating best practices between USAID programs and offices without mentioning the powerful role that civil society organizations can play in managing and mitigating conflicts.

U.S. aid shifted to the Middle East, especially to Egypt and Israel. It has recently, especially since 9/11, expanded to South and West Asia, especially Pakistan, Afghanistan, and Iraq. Aid policy must now shift to deepen involvement and connections in these and many other countries.

One of the great virtues of society-based initiatives is that they can be used not just in countries "friendly" to the United States, such as Indonesia, Iraq, Afghanistan, Pakistan, Palestine, Colombia, and Uganda; they can also be used—or start to be used—in countries like Syria, Iran, and possibly even North Korea. They can also provide an opening to progress in societies that are emerging from civil or ethnic conflict in Africa and Latin America, as well as in many countries that are still caught up in conflict.

Giving priority to society-based initiatives will add crucial economic, political, and social development instruments to foreign policymaking. Without these instruments and limited to state-based interventions, the United States and its allies will face choices between extreme positions and limited possibilities for success. The sterile dance between Europe and the United States over what to do about Iran's nuclear program is a perfect example of what happens when there are only "good cop/bad cop," state-focused choices.

Despite wide agreement and much rhetoric about the need to address development issues in new ways, real change is slow in happening. Aid budgets since 9/11, although larger, reflect little change in spending priorities. New initiatives such as the Middle East Partnership Initiative (MEPI) have been accorded low priority and are under-funded. Disappointment over MEPI is now leading to the consideration of creating a new, independent organization to support the Middle East modeled on The Asia Foundation. The new organization could support civil society and engage in advocacy on institutional and policy issues.

Although policymakers are constantly debating how to strengthen U.S. foreign assistance programs, and while they are in a continual learning process, they have not, until now, established development policies and priorities that would contribute strategically to post-Cold War foreign policy.

To achieve this goal, the government's development agencies, Congress, country missions, and the development "industry" must work together to make a strategic foreign assistance program a reality.

Civil Society as a Strategic Resource

CSOs that do this kind of work jealously guard their independence. It is thus a mistake to say that U.S. foreign policy can "recruit" them as partners or to give the impression that they can be "used" to promote U.S. foreign policy. The heart of our argument is the opposite of this: it is not that foreign policy should try to pull CSOs away from their missions, but that foreign policy should embrace and support many key CSO objectives. The main point is that where the objectives of a CSO and U.S. foreign policy overlap—which is the case in the examples we present in this essay and on many other issues— foreign policymakers should support them. Our argument is directed mainly to the government: to embrace these objectives, respecting CSO's independence, which is their greatest asset and the essential catalyst for the success of their endeavors throughout the world. Beyond the *reality* of independence is the central issue of *perception*. On this point a paradox looms large: The more independent the funding institution of the government is perceived to be, the greater the possibilities for strategic impact. When the State Department announces a new democracy program in Iran (for example), it paints targets on everyone who gets money under the program.

CSOs mediate between individuals and the state, often providing protection against authoritarian and totalitarian regimes, and often challenging them. They play a similar role in relation to religion and religious authorities, especially in Muslim countries. CSOs often provide the most powerful means of effecting economic, political, and social change in developing countries. Perhaps most importantly, they strengthen democratic institutions and culture by facilitating citizen self-governance in helping address a wide range of economic, social, and political issues. These multiple functions explain why building and supporting strong civil societies needs to be a new priority in promoting change. Its importance is especially obvious in reviewing the conditions that promote terrorists and terrorism.

Many people argue that poverty is not a cause of terrorism, citing as evidence the nineteen middle class and well-educated terrorists who hijacked the planes on 9/11. However, we believe that both objective causes (such as poverty and unemployment) and subjective causes (alienation and humiliation) are important and need to be addressed. While terrorist leaders who do spectacular acts may be middle class, the feelings of alienation and humiliation widely shared in failed societies, especially by young men, provide support, safety, and recruits to the cause. Moreover, the failure of societies—economically and politically—is almost certainly a key ingredient in engendering their feelings of alienation and humiliation.[7]

The objective problems of poverty, unemployment, and political disempowerment are obvious enough. Subjective aggravations of humiliation and alienation are less obvious and need

7. The leading proponent of this view for the Arab countries is Bernard Lewis.

to be illustrated. All recent proposals for Middle East peace provide examples in focusing on the objective concerns of land for peace. While these objective issues are important, none of these proposals addresses the Palestinians' subjective feelings of humiliation and victimhood, and their demand for honor and respect. Yet many people close to the conflict insist these subjective needs represent their overriding concerns. Understanding these subjective needs forces a very different understanding of the challenge of peace in the region.

The problem of alienation and rootlessness—which involves the absence of a feeling of belonging to normal communities— was evident in most, if not all, of the terrorists who hijacked the planes on 9/11. Although many of the terrorists lived in the west, they had never integrated into the societies in which they lived. Instead they gravitated toward clerics on the fringes of the Muslim community who preached hatred of the west and the United States. All were also without stable long-term connections to women and girls both in their countries of origin and in the west.

The remedies for the objective challenges are economic and political development. The remedies for the subjective challenges are empowerment and connection (which is also empowering). Unlike governments, which specialize in providing for objective public needs, CSOs specialize in empowering and connecting citizens. Many communities participating in the World Bank's initiative promoting community "ownership" of schools in Baluchistan (Pakistan) in the 1990s consistently resisted and opposed religious fundamentalism.[8] This has also been true for the two largest Muslim organizations in Indonesia, working with the Asia Foundation (TAF) to build a moderate, tolerant Islamic democracy in that country.[9] CSOs address the subjective causes

8. Barbara Herz, interview by A. Lawrence Chickering, January 30, 2006.
9. William P. Fuller, President of TAF from 1989–2004, interview by A. Lawrence Chickering, Sept. 9, 2005.

of terrorism in powerful ways while also addressing problems of poverty and education.

When CSOs work with governments, they can often produce the most strategically important accomplishments in addressing economic or political issues. In any area of public policy—for example, economic policy reform, institutional and legal reform, voter registration and education, early childhood and formal education, environmental and health policy, and formal peace negotiations—CSOs can play crucial roles in encouraging governments to "own" a reform proposal. On other issues, especially involving community mobilization and empowerment, CSOs can play the dominant role in empowering and connecting people, with little initial involvement of governments. However, the pace of reform and change can greatly accelerate when CSOs work with government ministry staffs to help facilitate and encourage community mobilization to strengthen civil society.

Local Ownership of the Need to Change

Positive change occurs best and becomes sustainable when there is "local ownership"—when people and governments are committed to change and participate in development activities. Local ownership means different things in different issue areas. In the case of economic policy reform, the ownership that is important is by government policymakers and by economic and political community leadership groups. In the case of girls' education and women's empowerment, authority figures—typically fathers but also local tribal leaders in traditional, rural areas—must accept the ideas. In educational reform, ownership must be embraced by provincial ministerial offices of education, by local CSOs, by teachers, communities, and parents as well as by the ministries of education and finance.

Leadership by local CSOs in all of these areas helps assure local ownership. This has been shown in society-based initiatives on economic policy reform, legal and regulatory reform, in strategies promoting education reform (especially girls' education and the empowerment of women), and in recruiting citizens as partners in the search for peace. This is true even in the most "difficult" countries and even during civil strife. These changes have included basic shifts in attitudes toward women in highly traditional regions of Arab countries and greatly reduced hostility toward enemies in conflicts marked by hatred and fear. In every case, the key was successful promotion of local ownership of the need to change by local CSOs.

One of the most important keys to promoting local ownership is avoiding foreign, especially U.S. government, authorship. The most powerful authority for local action is local. Local civil society is often the most powerful avenue to local ownership even if it is government officials that need to "own" a commitment to change. Typically, however, government officials are not enough; other non-governmental leadership groups—larger circles of influence—are also important to strengthen and sustain the commitment to change, especially when governments change.

Although there are many documented strategies for building local ownership of education reform (for instance), sometimes these are forgotten or ignored, especially where there is high-level, political support for action. A prominent example is state-to-state U.S. efforts to promote education reform in Arab countries. These efforts are foundering principally because insufficient attention has been given to civil society and its potential for generating local ownership in reform processes.

Promoting Strategic
Development Policies

USAID missions, in developing their country strategies, aim to be strategic in allocating funds budgeted for each country. They do so, however, under the shadow of a variety of powerful constraints that limits their authority to make effective and balanced country plans. The most important of these is congressional mandates ("earmarks") about how to spend the money for certain sectors in the country or across the region. Critics charge that congressional earmarks, which control more than 80 percent of USAID's budget, are just congressional pork given to special interest groups. We believe, however, that they are a symptom of a deeper disease. The deeper problem is the failure of foreign policymakers to establish more compelling criteria for allocating foreign assistance. To reduce congressional earmarks, foreign policymakers must provide compelling reasons for spending aid money on certain strategies and not others. The best way to do this is to design a development policy that contributes strategically to U.S. and international security. Only such a policy, emphasizing strategic value, has a chance of reducing congressional earmarks.

At present, the overriding strategic principle in foreign assistance allocates funds to *countries* judged to be important: Egypt and Israel are obvious examples, and secondarily to a few *sectors* (not strategies). Given the changed nature of the threat to U.S. and international security and development, funding ought to be allocated especially to *strategic programs* directed at priority countries, which would include weak and even hostile, undemocratic states.[10]

10. Some states are both economically and politically failed (Syria, Sudan). Some are at risk of failing (Pakistan). Still others may appear strong and to some degree successful but are failing politically, generating widespread dis-

We recognize that recent foreign assistance policy has focused on investing in democratic, open-market societies and that support has been withdrawn for education, health, and other human development programs in countries led by dictators, corrupt politicians, and militant governments. Many of those countries, however, are precisely the places where millions of children and parents are suffering from severe poverty, unemployed youth are becoming increasingly militant, and terrorists are building new training camps. In the face of those realities, small indications are appearing of interest in reexamining this policy. We hope this reexamination will lead to increasing, nuanced support for national CSOs working in strategic areas.

Society-Based
Interventions That Work

Many examples exist of initiatives that promote the kind of society-wide changes we believe are essential to protecting American and international security. In the chapters that follow we offer brief analyses of initiatives to promote economic policy reform, property rights for the poor, education for girls and empowerment of women, recruitment of citizens in the search for peace, strategies for nation-building, and the key roles CSOs can play during and after conflicts.

We are not suggesting these are the only programs that can contribute effectively to a strategic foreign aid program. Many programs run by CSOs could support such an approach, including legal reform initiatives, legal aid, voter surveys and educa-

---

content (Egypt, Saudi Arabia). In mentioning these examples, we are not suggesting the answer is always strategic aid, for this, obviously, is not appropriate for a country like Saudi Arabia. However, the Saudi example is a large threat to national and international security; and strategies to address it need to be developed.

tion, environmental research and advocacy, early childhood and formal and non-formal education, health and nutrition, moderate Islamic associations, "peoples' assemblies" to generate popular support and legitimacy for large, constitutional reforms, and others. We have chosen to focus on certain issues as *examples* of what can be done. We have also chosen them because we think there will be widespread agreement about their strategic value. These kinds of interventions address both the objective and subjective causes and conditions that promote terrorism, while they also enhance economic, social, and political development.

Economic policy reform and capitalizing the poor, mitigate poverty and unemployment. Capitalizing the poor also empowers people—especially the poor—to control their own lives. Educating girls and empowering adult women address the challenge of connection: bringing women as peacemakers into prominent view in societies, reducing the isolation of many young men who have little contact with women. Educating girls through community-based schools reconnects and empowers individuals and communities, while creating the conditions for women's economic and political empowerment.

Recruiting citizens as partners in peace empowers citizens and mitigates self-perceptions of one side or the other as powerless "victims" because it brings the disputants together under conditions of mutual respect. Connecting people in building cultures of peace also reduces the sense of rootlessness. These generalizations about citizens and peace also hold for civil society strategies in post-conflict societies as they connect, engage, and empower people. Connection is important for all human beings, and in healthy societies people's connections are manifold and complex—personal, familial, artistic, recreational, religious, political. Multiple connections limit the danger that a person—political or religious, for example—will become obsessive and extreme. To make the point in relation to Muslim countries (and quoting Richard Haass, president of the Council on Foreign Relations), it is important that the mosque not be the only mediating institution outside the family. Multiple connections through multiple civil society organizations enrich people's lives and represent a crucial institutional foundation for societies searching for democracy.

All programs that facilitate civic engagement and build trust help to mitigate religious hatred. They bring people together, reduce isolation, and promote non-violent resolution of conflicts. Finally, where community mobilization is used to promote girls' education, or any other social reform, it has been shown to open traditional fathers' sense of possibility for their daughters and to effect profound changes in (formerly fundamentalist) attitudes toward their patriarchal norms.[11]

Changing how people think often requires showing it is possible to change how they live. Mobilizing and training people to solve their own problems multiplies the impact of reforms and operates at high scales and low cost. Some of the programs and issue areas we have selected address rather conventional objectives of public policy reform, such as economic policy reform achieved through central government action. Others involve more unconventional objectives, especially in the areas of social transformation and political reform including empowerment of women through grass roots community mobilization and recruitment of citizens in the search for peace.

11. This is based on interviews with Malak Zaalouk, director of education programs for UNICEF in Egypt, and about the impacts of the Girls' Community Schools around the city of Asyut in Upper Egypt and also with Carol Morris, of the British Council, for many schools in Northwest Pakistan. It is also based on the interview with Greg Mortenson on Pakistan.

Toward Strategic
Foreign Assistance

The first priority in designing a strategic development program is for policymakers to focus on building civil society in the countries that are the greatest threats to U.S. security. While policymakers may choose other programs or may add to our list, we encourage them to stay focused and not try to do everything:

Step One: Select a Short List of Strategic Actions

Being strategic means being focused. Current aid programs try to do everything, but doing everything makes it hard to achieve real (strategic) impact. We propose focusing on the following issues, and relying on interventions that have been demonstrated to work:

1. Reforming economic policy and capitalizing the poor;
2. Educating girls and empowering women;
3. Recruiting citizens to work for peace;
4. Engaging citizens in nation building: encouraging people to look beyond sectarian and tribal loyalties; and
5. Supporting CSOs during and after conflicts and in fragile states that are vulnerable to future conflict.

Step Two: Select Four or Five Priority Countries
and Prepare Country Strategic Plans for Each

Priority countries should be those of greatest importance to U.S. and international security. Afghanistan, Iran, Iraq, Pakistan, Palestine, and Syria might be good places to start. At a minimum, we would then add Colombia and Sudan, and rapidly expand support to key countries in sub-Saharan Africa, Latin America, and other world regions experiencing conflicts or working on post-conflict nation building. The fact that several of these are societies in conflict should not be a barrier to engaging CSOs in maintaining fragile infrastructure for eventual social and economic reconstruction—as well as promoting reduced conflict. Finally, it is important immediately to start looking for opportunities to build civil society and work in North Korea.

The Country Strategic Plans should focus on a few strategic objectives in these countries. They should propose activities that would accomplish significant economic, educational, political, or social change. The objectives can be long-term, such as educating girls or empowering women, or shorter-term, such as developing informal channels of communication for dialogue about key development activities with opposition groups (Sunni groups in Iraq, secular democratic groups and the Muslim Brotherhood in Egypt). However, in thinking about timeframes, *perceptions* often play an important role in strategic change, and perceptions can change more quickly than reality.

In Step One we have suggested some priority objectives, and other possible priorities will undoubtedly arise during preparation of the Country Strategic Plans.

Step Three: Create Special Funds to Finance the Country Plans and to Promote Civil Society

Separate budgets for a limited number of strategic priorities would focus the effort. It would connect the commitment and funding to the priorities.

The Issue of Cost

One of the key elements in strategic investments is cost. Many USAID programs cannot have broad cumulative effects because as currently designed, they are too costly to implement on a national or multinational scale. However, the activities we are recommending here—advocacy of institutional, economic, and political reform, empowerment of people, engagement of citizens as partners in development, and peace-making and nation-building during and after conflicts—are all relatively inexpensive compared to other parts of a development budget. In the Appendix, we provide an estimate of a budget for a hypothetical country program (for Pakistan) to illustrate estimated general costs. Our purpose in sketching this hypothetical program is to show how small the costs would be in terms of strategic foreign assistance compared to other parts of the development budget and the military budget.

The problem of cost raises a final issue about the importance of committing to a serious program of research and development. R & D is no less important in political and social interventions than it is in weapons development. The United States government spends billions of dollars in researching and developing new weapons. As we come to see these society-based economic, educational, and political initiatives as strategic, it will be obvious that we need to invest just as seriously in developing and testing new models for these initiatives. This is especially true in developing political strategies for promoting economic, social, and political reforms. And it is also, finally, important in developing approaches to reduce costs so that interventions can be mounted on scales that are strategic.

Conclusion

The emergence of the societies and economies of some countries as threats to U.S. and international security presents large challenges to U.S. foreign policy. Organizing and managing effective sources of information is difficult enough in relation to states. It is enormously more difficult in relation to societies and the invisible adversaries they shelter. Existing foreign policy and intelligence agencies struggle to address the new reality for precisely the same reason that planned and centralized economies are helpless to operate complex, modern economies. As Friedrich Hayek and Milton Friedman argued, limited economic knowledge about the market created the need for hundreds of millions of market participants in a market economy. Collectivist approaches that relied on thousands of central planners were overwhelmed and unable to acquire enough knowledge to act effectively. Similar limits of knowledge in the new world of foreign policy require the participation of thousands of innovators within CSOs of troubled societies who alone have the capacity to understand the new realities they and their countrymen face.

The only way for foreign policymakers to overcome the information deficit they face in dealing with failed and fragile states is to work with citizens and citizen-based organizations in other countries as partners in addressing multiple challenges, especially in those places that have become security threats. In a new policy environment, local civil society organizations could become the most important partners of the United States and other democratic nations because of their advantages of language, culture, sensibility, ethnicity, local relationships, and trust.

2. Economic Development

Civil society organizations (CSOs) have played a variety of different roles in promoting economic development. This chapter examines three of them. First, we look at the International Center for Economic Growth (ICEG), which, from 1986 to 1995, promoted economic policy reform through a network of policy institutes in more than a hundred countries. Second is the Instituto Libertad y Democracia (ILD), based in Lima, Peru, which promotes institutional reform promoting property rights for the poor; and third, we look at the Orangi Project, a community-based, self-help project that builds and maintains a variety of infrastructure projects supporting a poor, urban neighborhood of several million in Karachi, Pakistan.

International Center for Economic Growth (ICEG)

Promotion of sound economic policies has been an objective of U.S. foreign policy in developing countries for more than three decades. In 2005, the reason is fairly obvious. Most of the world's greatest trouble spots, including many of the countries that harbor terrorists, have failed and closed economies, widespread poverty, poor health, low educational levels, little opportunity for women, environmental devastation, often high birth rates, and little hope. While failed economies are not the only cause of these problems, weak economies contribute to all of them.

Countries with the worst performing economies are primarily the "failed" and fragile states that include several strategic priorities, both past and proposed: pre-invasion Afghanistan, Egypt, Iran, pre-invasion Iraq, Sudan, and others. All have or had closed economies and limited economic contact with other countries. Corruption is also a serious problem in most of them—demoralizing people and encouraging revolutionaries and terrorists.

Open economies are essential to promote development and create opportunity. Other economic reforms can play an important role in reducing corruption and creating the sense that a society is fair and just. The long-term gains from economic policy reform are considerable. So why is it so difficult to accomplish? The reason is because powerful interest groups, who stand to lose with reform, block it.

The challenge is to promote reform without generating opposition and even hostility. The key to reform is local ownership and support, which instills confidence that reform will bring the promised long-term benefits. One reason large international organizations, including USAID, have had trouble promoting reform is that they have not been able to achieve local ownership of the need for reform.

A powerful model exists for achieving local ownership and promoting reform in the experience of the International Center for Economic Growth (ICEG). Between 1986 and 1995 ICEG enjoyed considerable success helping build institutional capacity in economic research organizations to promote economic reform in developing and transitional countries.

ICEG was directed and run by economists in Latin America but with Ph.Ds from American universities. ICEG played a major role in promoting significant market-oriented reforms in more than fifty countries during this ten-year period. It did this by supporting a network of more than 300 economic policy institutes in more than 110 countries—financing research grants and networking them to promote "south-south learning."

To some degree, ICEG accomplished local ownership of reform in its very structure as a global network of affiliates run by economists in developing countries. Starting in Latin America, the network and program expanded to Asia, Central Europe, the Middle East, and finally Sub-Saharan Africa.

With primary support from USAID, ICEG was founded in 1986, the year after Gorbachev came to power in the Soviet Union. The founders wanted it to be directed by someone from a developing country; and Nicolas Ardito-Barletta, former President of Panama and former Vice President of the World Bank, became the first General Director. For more than nine years the organization's headquarters were therefore in Panama City, with its operational office in San Francisco.

Barletta, who got his Ph.D. in economics from the University of Chicago, brought with him a network of U.S.-trained economists throughout the hemisphere—from Chicago, MIT, Yale, Stanford, Harvard, and other leading schools.

In its early years, ICEG focused on three objectives: building its network of affiliates, developing a publication program with an "inventory of knowledge" for policy leaders, and launching a research program that gave grants to its affiliates supporting research aimed at promoting major policy reforms.

The network expanded very rapidly. Although ICEG had a decidedly pro-market orientation, reflecting the mainstream orientation of the economics profession, it applied no ideological test in selecting affiliates. It opened its membership to any institution that wanted to participate in an open global dialogue on development.

The commitment to reach across ideological boundaries was important because it meant that ICEG could work with one institute close to the governing party in a country, while also working with the institute advising the opposition party. This mode of operation allowed for considerable continuity in policy even when the country's leadership changed. The standard was professional, not ideological.

Between 1986 and 1995 ICEG published more than forty full-length books and dozens of monographs, country studies, and occasional papers on issues ranging from tax, trade, and regulatory reform to market approaches to environmental policy and human development. The publications, which were of the highest professional standard, were written by both international scholars and scholars and policymakers from developing countries. ICEG published these in English and also translated many of them into a number of languages, including Arabic, Chinese, French, Portuguese, Russian, Spanish, and others.

ICEG authors included many of the best known names working on development—from Nobel Laureates (Theodore W. Schultz, Sir Arthur Lewis, Douglass North, Joseph Stiglitz, and Lawrence Klein) to developing country scholars and policymakers (Domingo Cavallo, Carlos Langoni, Leopoldo Solis, Mohamed Sadli, and many others) to leading contemporary thinkers (Richard N. Cooper, Anne O. Krueger, Ronald I. McKinnon, Jeffrey Sachs, T. Paul Schultz, and T.N. Srinivasan).

Research Grants

One of ICEG's first and most important programs was grants awarded to its member institutes supporting policy research focused on unusual opportunities to produce real reform. ICEG's grant on trucking regulation in Mexico shows the potential of these grants. ICEG awarded it to two young Mexican economists, Arturo Fernandez and Francisco Gil Diaz (who is the country's current Finance Minister), who concluded that the trucking industry was a corrupt and inefficient cartel. The entire industry was owned by twelve families, none of whom owned a single truck. They owned the government's *permission* to operate trucks, and they in turn leased their permission to others, who paid them handsome bounties for the privilege.

Fernandez and Gil Diaz proposed deregulating the industry, allowing free entry for anyone who could pass simple requirements. The twelve families lost their monopoly, and the reform was estimated to save the Mexicans one billion dollars per year and reduced the cost of trucking substantially. The study also provided a powerful demonstration of one strategy for reducing corruption.

ICEG also sponsored special, targeted projects aimed at particular objectives: a special dialogue between Latin American economists and the Catholic Bishops Conference on "Development and the Social Doctrine of the Church"; a six-country study on "Military Spending and Development," bringing together economists and generals to explore how excessive weapons spending reduces economic growth and makes countries poorer; and a six-country study of water pollution in Latin America.

ICEG was also instrumental in getting Myrna Levant, the leader of FUSADES, an influential think tank in El Salvador and an ICEG affiliate, to recruit Arnold Harberger and a team of Chileans to prepare the strategy and the policy reform package for the government of Alfredo Cristiani in El Salvador. The package started the reconstruction program, which has continued through several phases to the present time.

Some ICEG programs played an important role in reducing conflict and promoting democratic collaboration. In El Salvador, before the 1994 elections, ICEG helped organize a conference sponsored by one of its affiliates and supported by all of them, bringing together business, labor, political leaders, and CSOs to talk about the importance of sound economic policies to social progress. Among the participants were seven former guerrilla leaders who had created a new political party. The candidates for vice president of the two major parties were featured speakers.

In 1990 ICEG held its first regional meeting outside Latin America, in Bangkok, for its Asian affiliates. The program became active in Central Europe during the turbulent period after 1989, and it was also very active in the early 1990s in India, working through seven affiliates, supporting the government's trade reform initiative with both research and public education.

Once it started working outside Latin America, ICEG began inviting participants to meetings from other regions, to facilitate interregional learning. One affiliate in the Dominican Republic, for example, created a service analyzing the economic impact of bills pending before that country's legislature. Other institutes started imitating the practice, and similar services appeared in several other Latin American countries and also in the Philippines.

Besides its research grants, ICEG also sponsored special seminars on communication, training its affiliates in strategies for communicating their research results to policy leaders.

As a result of these activities and with a core budget that never exceeded $2.5 million, between 1986 and 1995 ICEG played a significant role in promoting major policy reforms in more than fifty countries.[1]

1. In its first three years, when it was working only in Latin America, ICEG's core budget from USAID was only $800,000 a year. In 1989, when it expanded to Asia and Central Europe, the core budget increased to $2.5 million. With other sources of funding, its total funding probably averaged about $3.5 million and never exceeded $4 million in any year.

Lessons on Establishing Local Ownership and Building In-Country Capacity

ICEG's experience reveals some important things about the challenge of promoting local ownership of international ideas. First, it recalls the value of well-trained people, financed in the past by fellowship programs for Ph.Ds in economics from U.S. (or European) universities. The best-known examples are the "Chicago Boys," who managed the highly successful economic reforms in Chile over the past two decades, and the "Berkeley Mafia," who effectively guided Indonesian economic policies for more than two decades after 1966.

The importance of professional training is especially evident in Latin America. Since the 1970s, U.S.-trained economists at the Ph.D. level have increasingly become ministers of economy, finance, and planning and also heads of Central Banks and other key positions in Latin American governments.[2] They are responsible for the wave of economic reforms that increased in the 1980s and 1990s—making careers for Ph.Ds who moved back and forth between think tanks and government policy positions. This is true not only in all Latin American countries, but also

---

2. To give some examples, in Mexico under President Salinas more than six cabinet members had Ph.D.s in economics from U.S. universities: Harvard, MIT, Stanford, Berkeley, Yale, and Chicago. Six deputy ministers were from Chicago. Ernesto Zedillo, who was president after Salinas and democratized the political system, has a Yale Ph.D. The present Minister of Finance, Francisco Gil Diaz, got his Ph.D. from Chicago. Miguel de la Madrid, the former President, went to Harvard.

In Latin America there are more than 800 Ph.D.s in economics from U.S. universities. At one time half of them came from the program that Arnold Harberger ran at Chicago with the Catholic University in Santiago. But it is not only in Latin America. In Indonesia, Mohammad Sadli and a whole group of his colleagues have Berkeley Ph.D.s. In Singapore, a number of leading economists have Ph.D.s from Berkeley and Stanford.

in Asia Pacific countries including Indonesia, Korea, Singapore, and Thailand.

Programs supporting Ph.D. training in the United States were financed primarily by USAID and the Ford Foundation going back to the 1950s. There were a plethora of fellowship programs in many countries, and they built a large human infrastructure of well-trained technicians. These investments had enormous strategic impact even though anecdotes from the time suggest that some of them were undertaken with limited strategic intentions.[3]

The Rockefeller Foundation was one of the first U.S. institutions to launch a major capacity-building initiative aimed at bringing technology and training to a developing country. The foundation's major focus was a program it founded in Mexico from 1942 to 1965 supporting fellowships for masters and Ph.D. training and research to develop new varieties of wheat and corn. The program trained 180 graduate students, including ninety Ph.Ds. Rockefeller's Norman Borlaug eventually took the program to India, where it produced the Green Revolution. He won the Nobel Peace Prize for it in 1970.[4]

Think tanks and universities have played an important role

3. In 1967 a fortuitous meeting between Barletta and Walt W. Rostow, President Johnson's National Security Advisor, led to the financing of fifty or sixty economic fellowships in Panama, including some for masters and some for Ph.D. training. Panama's current Minister of Finance, as well as the Deputy Minister of Finance, received their graduate training under that program. Then in 1983, when Marxist insurgencies were emerging in El Salvador and Nicaragua, officials at the World Bank met with Henry Kissinger, who was heading a special commission to develop a Central American initiative under President Reagan. That program included fellowships for graduate economics training from those two countries to counter training of Salvadorans and Nicaraguans by the Cubans.

4. Nicolas Ardito-Barletta, "Costs and Social Benefits of Agricultural Research in Mexico," Ph.D. dissertation, University of Chicago, 1971.

in every country that has enjoyed strong economic and social progress. It is particularly true in Asia, where large public-private institutions, such as the Korean Development Institute (KDI) in South Korea, have been supported on a scale sufficient to ensure that development policies are informed by the highest quality research.[5]

With the end of the Cold War, interest in these strategic investments declined, and they have not been sustained in many parts of the world. Most of the international fellowship programs of USAID and several foundations have been steeply curtailed in favor of short-term in-country or third country training in an attempt especially to reduce brain drain and lower training costs. However, both international fellowships and in-country and third country training are needed. It is time to reconsider current international training policies because clearly all was not lost in brain drain, and many development objectives were achieved through preparing nations' top leaders. Building bridges between nations through cooperative training and university partnership programs should be revitalized—this time with strong Internet linkages between institutions of higher education throughout the world.

Promoting Economic Reform

Building local capacity that can provide leadership for reform—both in terms of people and institutions—is central to promoting economic reform. Three components are needed to develop this capacity: building technical capacity, through fellowship programs for Ph.D. and masters degrees either in the U.S. or in developing countries; support of high quality institutions capable

5. Sylvia Ostry, ed., *Authority and Academic Scribblers: The Role of Research in East Asian Policy Reform* (San Francisco: ICS Press, 1991).

of doing good policy research and advocacy; and finally, support of an international institution or institutions, like ICEG, that can network the institutions in different countries so they can learn from each other, provide training, award research contracts, and oversee their quality.

Most important is building local capacity—people and institutions—that can provide leadership for reform. A successful program needs both well-trained individuals and institutions.

One priority should be funding of fellowships for Ph.D. and masters programs. Ph.D. students cost roughly $50,000 a year each for at least four years for a total of $200–250,000 each. Masters students cost perhaps half that. Training programs in other countries cost much less and might help reduce brain drain. Another antidote to brain drain would be to finance institutions to enable them to pay competitive wages to keep Ph.D.s in the country. The "right" scale for a program like this would emerge from experience.

We think that building an institution or institutions in target countries designed by professional economists in those countries is also important to improve economic policy. Such institutions exist in every country, but additional investments will often be needed to improve them. Even focusing on as many as ten priority countries, the cost of such a program would not exceed $15–20 million per year.[6] That seems a small price to pay, given the stakes we now face especially in failed and fragile states.

Finally, an international organization like ICEG—preferably run by developing country economists—should oversee quality, coordinate south-south learning, and organize networking that will permit sharing of experiences that are so important for learning how to improve performance. ICEG's core budget

---

6. This assumes ten new economists per year per country, which is far more than is practical in terms of finding good candidates in many countries.

never exceeded $2.5 million per year. In 1995, the USAID budget was cut substantially, the agency failed to renew its support, and ICEG's role as a global institution ended. We recommend that USAID consider providing support for a new organization capable of doing this kind of work, though on a greatly expanded scale, working in the priority regions of South and West Asia, the Middle East, Sub-Saharan Africa, and conflict-affected regions of Latin America. To build a new organization capable of working in these priority regions would require a budget of at least $10 million.

While a program with these three components would be costly, there is little question it would be extremely cost-effective in terms of improved economic performance, reduced poverty, increased employment, and other benefits associated with strong economies.

Capitalizing the Poor: Instituto Libertad y Democracia (Lima, Peru)

USAID has financed one civil society organization that did battle with a violent terrorist organization and won, using a unique strategy for empowering the poor. The CSO is an unusual think tank in Lima, Peru, called the Instituto Libertad y Democracia (ILD), founded and led by the charismatic Hernando de Soto. The terrorist organization was Sendero Luminoso (Shining Path), a violent Maoist organization with its political base among the country's rural peasants.

De Soto believed the war would be decided by a conflict of ideas. He argued that the central issue both for the poor and for development was and is property rights: security of ownership of real property and of businesses. He argued in his first (1986) book *El Otro Sendero* (*The Other Path*)—a title he chose as a direct challenge to the Shining Path—that Peru's poor are not a proletariat but entrepreneurs forced to live outside the law by an unresponsive legal system that imposes massive bureaucratic regulations on them. Fewer than 5 percent of Peruvian workers are employed by large businesses; the overwhelming majority own their own businesses. They own significant assets, and they represent a significant fraction both of Peru's population and its economy.

Although they are forced to work outside the law, "off-the-books," de Soto argues that these informal entrepreneurs have shown they want to live under the rule of law by making their own (informal) rules about property, what de Soto calls "extra-legal law."[7] He argues, in fact, that Peru's poor are the country's real entrepreneurs, in contrast to much of its traditional business sector, which lives off government favors given by its "mercantilist" system. The class struggle, then, is not between Marx's proletariat and business; it is between people who live off government favors and people who are excluded from the formal system.

De Soto estimated the size of the informal sector by walking the streets and shantytowns of Peru, talking to people about their work and counting their businesses. What he discovered was not the marginal workforce described by the government and by elites, but a class of entrepreneurs doing essential work for Peru's economy. He found in the informal sector:

- 90 percent of all small industrial enterprises,

- 85 percent of urban transport,

- 60 percent of Peru's fishing fleet (one of the biggest in the world), and

7. The best summary of the ILD's history and its fight against Sendero Luminoso appears in de Soto's preface to the new edition of *The Other Path* (New York: Basic Books, 2002).

- 60 percent of grocery distributors.

He estimated that 60–80 percent of Peru's population operates outside the law.

De Soto describes the effect of having to live in the informal sector. Because they must operate outside the law, informal entrepreneurs therefore

> do not have access to the facilitative devices that a formal legal system should provide to help them organize and leverage resources. Because they have no secure property rights and cannot issue shares, they cannot capture investment. Because they have no patents or royalties, they cannot encourage or protect innovations. Because they do not have access to contracts and justice organized on a wide scale, they cannot develop long-term projects. Because they cannot legally burden their assets, they are unable to use their homes and businesses to guarantee credit.[8]

The ILD mounted a major public education program on why Peruvians would continue to have trouble generating wealth without a legal property system. The reasons are because "ownership cannot be certain, addresses cannot be systematically verified, assets cannot be described according to standard business practices, people cannot be made to pay their debts, [and perpetrators] of fraud . . . cannot be easily identified."

De Soto grew up in Geneva from the age of seven and returned to Peru thirty years later, after running a large engineering firm in Europe. When he started doing business in Peru, he realized it was much more difficult than in Europe. Wondering why, he hired students to research the number of laws and regulations enacted in Peru since World War II. He found that Peru was passing nearly 30,000 laws and regulations a year regulating how citizens produce and distribute wealth. He con-

8. Ibid.

cluded that this mass of regulations provided few real benefits to most people.

De Soto founded the ILD in the early 1980s to promote reform of legal and regulatory structures that obstruct the poorest people from participating in market economies and even from participating as full citizens in their societies. De Soto's first study looked at the red tape facing people who tried to register a simple business. He found it took 289 days working eight hours a day—in addition to multiple bribes. Since this amounted to thirty-one times the average monthly minimum wage, the poor could not afford to operate legally, so they worked outside the law, buying protection with bribes, but with the constant insecurity that the law could come down on them at any time.

The moment de Soto chose the provocative title for his book, he knew he was at war with a movement that had killed thousands of innocent people. So he hired a bodyguard, bullet-proofed his car, and wore a bullet-proof vest. He didn't have to wait long. One bomb attack killed three people and injured nineteen at the ILD offices. But in the end his ideas proved to be the more powerful weapons.

In 1991, the ILD started registering property rights for coca farmers in Peru's northern jungle areas. In gratitude—and presumably because they didn't like dealing with terrorists—the farmers started giving the government information on how to drive the terrorists and drug traffickers out of the area. De Soto notes that during this period Peru's participation in the international cocaine market began to decline from 60 percent to 25 percent. The founder of the Shining Path, Abimael Guzman, was driven out of the countryside into Lima, where authorities arrested him in 1993. His organization has ceased to function today.

De Soto's book, which focuses on Peru, became an instant

best-seller in Peru and throughout Latin America. De Soto became a hero to the poor, working in the informal sector—unconnected and alienated from society. His campaign to extend property rights to the poor found strong support across the political spectrum. If Milton Friedman supported him from the beginning, Bill Clinton is one of his greatest supporters today. Even the Marxist candidate for President of Peru, Alphonso Barantes, said in the early 1990s that he wanted de Soto as his running mate. From its beginning in Peru, de Soto's campaign has spread to all regions of the world. His second book has been translated into more than twenty languages and has sold more than a million copies.[9] Today he is working with more than thirty heads of state.

Besides their study of registration red tape, the ILD also simulated the registration process for getting title to untitled land. They estimated the process in Peru would take six years and eleven months, working six hours a day—going through 205 bureaucratic steps. Everywhere it is working, the ILD today focuses on registering titles to land and businesses.

A New Kind of Think Tank

The ILD is an unusual kind of think tank. It specializes in identifying bottlenecks in legal and regulatory systems, and looks for opportunities to simplify legal processes. In economists' terms, the ILD is committed to reducing the "transactions costs" associated with doing business, especially for the poor. It is a unique action-research program, which exercises unusual influence in the political life of Peru. One reason for its success is de Soto's extraordinary talent for rallying public opinion to support ILD initiatives.

9. Hernando de Soto, *The Mystery of Capital: Why Capitalism Triumphs in the West and Fails Everywhere Else* (New York: Basic Books, 2000).

The ILD process only works in countries where it has political support from the highest officials in a country. The ILD
works in response to invitations from heads of state. It works
through a multi-step process that begins with researching the
extent of what de Soto calls "dead capital" (capital that has no
legal owner). The ILD's findings in Peru about the importance
of the informal sector, their asset holdings, and bureaucratic ex-
clusion are the same in many countries.[10]

The ILD presents these findings to heads of state through
elaborate, multi-colored maps. The maps highlight the potential
for increasing the value of underutilized resources and also for
helping the poor at very low cost, and their studies of regulatory
barriers to property rights lead naturally to strategies for legal
and regulatory reform. Public support for expanding opportunity overwhelms any bureaucratic resistance to eliminating the
barriers.

Once the legal barriers are removed, an enormous job remains to grant titles. The cost of titling is the most expensive
part of the process, but financing is already in place through
multilateral donors to do this. What is needed is core funding
to maintain the ILD's basic operation and early stage activities.

De Soto's experience involves a weak example of local ownership of ideas. His program has proven compelling even without local fingerprints on it. However, learning from another developing country is the next thing to ownership that is truly
local.

10. In Egypt, for example, the ILD has estimated that 88 percent of all
businesses in the country are informal and 92 percent of the housing. The
team also studies the bureaucratic impediments to achieving secure property
rights. Everywhere these impediments are similar to the situation in Peru:
dozens of bureaucratic steps engaging dozens of government agencies, often
with enormous fines imposed on squatters greatly exceeding the value of the
property. In Egypt, for example, registering a business took, on average, about
two years; and getting title to a home took about seventeen years.

Evaluating Impacts

While the ILD is now working in ten countries, its early work
in Peru has provided the most time and opportunities to observe
its impacts. Its formalization program began there in 1990 and
by July 1995 had assisted in formalizing 232,000 urban and rural
properties. In that time the ILD has estimated that the creation
of secure property rights increased property values between 60
and 250 percent, and additional improvements stimulated by
formalization further increased values 20 to 80 percent. Total
increases in property values, therefore, were between 80 and 330
percent.

The ILD also found a modest increase in the number of
mortgages and a substantial increase in the average size of loans:
from $1,500 in 1993 to $5,000 in 1995.

More recently, Harvard economist Erica Field and colleagues have found the following impacts of Peru's formalization
program, initiated by the ILD but then subsequently taken over
by the Peruvian government[11]:

- The titling program, which by 2002 had reached 1.2 million
  urban households, caused a significant shift in employment
  outside the home, increasing household income. Before titling, insecure titles forced the wife to stay at home to pro-
  tect it. Titling increased total household work hours 17 percent and reduced by 50 percent work done inside the home.
  Moreover, titling caused a marked (28 percent) reduction in
  child labor as adult labor was substituted for child labor, and
  reduced child labor translated into increased education.

- Some increase was observed in loans resulting from titling,

11. See four working papers by Erica Field, 2003 and 2004—available at
http://www.rwj.harvard.edu/scholarsbio/field/field.htm.

but this effect is relatively weak (all coming from non-profit lenders).

- In some ways the most interesting effects involve impacts on fertility, on intra-household ownership rights, and on bargaining on intra-family decisions. Land titles are associated with significant reduction in annual birth rates (declining 3-5 percent). They increase the probability that women will appear as owners of property (increasing 25 percent), and with title women are more likely to participate in household decision-making.

Sebastian Galiani (Universidad de San Andres) and Ernesto Schargrodsky (Universidad Torcuato Di Tella) reached similar findings in studying the impacts of formalization in Argentina. Thanks to a natural experiment that allowed comparison of two groups with the same characteristics, they show that granting property rights produces significant impacts on housing investment, household size, and school performance, while they show weaker effects on labor income and access to credit markets. With property rights, people live in better housing, household size declines, and school performance and investments in education increase.[12]

Political Implications

The cover design of the first American edition of de Soto's second book foreshadowed in an eerie way the importance of his work in fighting terrorism.[13] The cover featured a picture of the twin towers in New York City, with three hooded mullahs look-

---

12. Sebastian Galiani and Ernesto Schargrodsky, "The Effects of Land Titling," mimeo, 2005.

13. *The Mystery of Capital: Why Capitalism Triumphs in the West and Fails Everywhere Else*, 2000.

ing down at them from above. Despite the ILD's importance as a weapon against terrorism, U.S. foreign policymakers have made little effective effort to promote his work in strategically-important countries.[14] Pakistan provides an interesting example. In 2000 and 2001, before 9/11, private individuals tried to stimulate high-level government interest in bringing de Soto to Pakistan. They also tried to get the U.S. Embassy in Islamabad interested. These efforts went nowhere even after 9/11, when Pakistan overnight became a strategically important country. Then, in the spring of 2004, de Soto received a phone call from Islamabad. It was from the President of Pakistan, Pervez Musharraf, who said he had read *The Mystery of Capital* and wanted de Soto to come to Pakistan. The ILD is working in Pakistan because the country's president happened to read his book. Efforts to get him into Iraq and Afghanistan have failed, apparently for bureaucratic reasons.

In 2002, USAID made a decision not to renew its core support of about $2.5 million to the ILD. Strong bipartisan support in Congress continued funding, but reduced by 50 percent. The ILD now works on a direct, increased appropriation from Congress.

Importance to U.S. National Security

Formalization empowers individuals and families, while also formally connecting people to their legal systems and (therefore) their governments. Heretofore, about 90 percent of people in Egypt (for example) had no real connection to the Egyptian legal system—no connection to the state. Lack of connection is one

---

14. Although high level interest has appeared at various times to promote ILD work in strategically important countries like Afghanisan and Iraq, he is not actively involved in any country as a result of U.S. government efforts. The reason, presumably, is bureaucratic impediments.

reason why Egypt is today a fragile state and fertile ground for radical Islam and for terrorists. Property rights establish an important connection, binding citizens to their country and to other citizens not related by family or tribe—thus increasing trust and reducing alienation.

Besides these effects, which support our security in many countries, the ILD may be relevant in helping solve perhaps the most troublesome foreign policy challenge: the Israeli-Palestinian conflict.

Since the second Intifada began in September 2000, Israel has destroyed thousands of Palestinian homes. The Israeli government justifies its actions on grounds of national security. Its claims of legality, however, arise because many Palestinians have no legal title to their homes. While formalization could not guarantee an end to this practice, it would erect legal barriers that could greatly reduce it. The U.S. should push both the Israeli government and the PNA to support formalization, thus contributing to reduced tensions and conflict.

Despite these benefits and despite the very large investments the U.S. has made financing development of the ILD model, U.S. foreign policymakers have played no effective role in encouraging the ILD to work in strategic ways in strategically important countries. Initial efforts should focus on the most strategic interventions: Afghanistan, Pakistan, Iraq, and the Palestinian territories. Beyond these would be other countries judged to be security risks.

The costs associated with supporting the ILD's model are extremely low because substantial funding for all but the background stage of the work is available from multilateral donors, especially the World Bank. We have estimated the costs of implementing a serious program in Pakistan at $20 million over five years. Add perhaps $1 million for public education to communicate news of the program to people in all parts of the country, and the result would be an initiative of great strategic value at a relatively small cost. The ILD's core budget to operate in all regions of the world is only $6 million per year. Any serious judgment of the strategic value of this program would suggest our investment in the ILD should be very much larger than that.

On September 13, 2005, the United Nations announced the formation of a new, international initiative promoting empowerment of the poor. Co-chaired by Madeleine Albright and de Soto, the newly-established High-Level Commission on Legal Empowerment of the Poor has a six-fold agenda. Its first two priorities are to promote "a broad reform agenda for legal inclusion and empowerment of the poor" and to explore strategies "to secure broader access to legal, fungible property rights over real and movable assets." A long list of world leaders have signed on in support. This United Nations initiative deserves strong support from the U.S. Government.

The Orangi Pilot Project:
Enabling the Poor

Just as de Soto understood that extending property rights to the poor greatly enhances their ability to produce and invest, other social entrepreneurs around the world have recognized the potential of even the most desperately impoverished communities to help themselves. The Orangi Pilot Project (OPP) in Pakistan is a powerful example of how a poor community, if given the right tools, can mobilize to tackle even significant infrastructure projects.

OPP began as a way to address the acute sanitation problems of a sprawling illegal settlement in Karachi, but has evolved into a strategy of development rooted in self-help and community-mobilization. The OPP approach to community involvement has since been replicated in dozens of Pakistani cities and applied to healthcare, family planning, and small loan programs around the country. It has also been adapted as a development model by groups in South Africa, Central Asia, Nepal, Sri Lanka, India, the Philippines, Cambodia, Vietnam, Japan, and even wealthy donor countries.[15]

OPP Breaks Down Barriers

In 1980, Orangi was Karachi's largest kachi abadi (illegal squatter settlement) with more than one million inhabitants. Orangi residents were mostly semi-skilled migrant workers who had moved to the city as laborers, clerks, and shopkeepers. Since Orangi fell outside the scope of the city master plan, authorities failed to provide any services to its population beyond the main roads, a few schools, and electricity lines. The government largely ignored the numerous petitions initiated by Orangi residents for a basic sewage system, and until 1980, most households used bucket latrines for the disposal of human waste.[16] Residents bore the physical costs associated with rotting garbage and fetid waste, and many contracted water borne diseases, such as malaria, typhoid, scabies, dysentery, and diarrhea.

Recognizing that the government was never going to help the residents of Orangi, Akhter Hamid Khan, an engineer and social scientist, believed he could organize the people to address their own problems. Khan, better known as Khansaheb, was a devoted Muslim who had served in the Indian Civil Service for many years. He brought a deep spirituality, respect for the poor, and exacting administrative skills to his social activism. The "basti (slum) dwellers," Khan noted, "want to survive and pros-

15. "Orangi—A Model in Community Self-Help," *Inter Press Service*, 10/22/99.
16. Ibid.

per. They are frugal, diligent, enterprising and resourceful. They are workers and producers, not free-loaders and spongers. They do not need doles and subsidies, secure jobs or free homes."[17] All they needed was some organization and technical expertise that he believed could be imparted cost-effectively.

Akhter Hamid Khan established the Orangi Pilot Project as a research institute to develop solutions that could be implemented by the local population. Orangi residents were well aware of their sewage-related issues, but prior to OPP's involvement, they felt the barriers facing them were too great to overcome. The cost of such a project seemed prohibitive, they were not organized to take collective action, and no one in the community had the technical expertise to undertake such a project.

Akhter Hamid Khan believed the Orangi community could overcome these obstacles. OPP research found that Orangi residents were willing and capable of tackling 90 percent of the construction and maintenance of a sewage system—including installing toilets inside their houses, connecting their houses to underground sewer lines, and building secondary collector drains. The main drains and treatment plant were beyond the limits of community action.

Khansaheb knew that the community had to be organized in groups small enough to encourage participation, but large enough to accomplish the huge task of building a sewage system. The people of Orangi, with OPP's assistance, decided to organize around their lanes (consisting of twenty to forty houses) and formed "lane committees." Each lane committee then elected lane managers, who went door to door and collected funds to buy materials and hire labor for their respective lanes.

In the decade following the start of the Orangi Pilot Project,

17. *Dawn*, October 12, 1999.

each Orangi household contributed an average of $34 to raise approximately $2 million. Various analyses show that community residents completed their work at one quarter to one eighth the cost of a conventional sewage system provided by government agencies. Cost effectiveness was achieved in large part through the community's voluntary labor.[18] By doing the work within the community, OPP was able to minimize the perennial problems of corruption, profiteering, and inefficiency.[19] Also, the work was based on simple and cost-effective technologies and designs that were identified by OPP research.[20]

Evaluating Impacts

As the Orangi community became more organized, it was able to apply collective pressure on municipal authorities to provide additional funding for primary and secondary sewer lines. Within a decade of the launch of OPP, 73 percent of Orangi's 6,347 lanes had sewer lines and 75 percent of the 94,122 houses had indoor sanitary latrines.[21] The result has been a substantial decline in sanitation-related diseases. Moreover, the skill base of community residents increased dramatically. Lane managers received important administrative and leadership experience, and many residents were trained in basic masonry and sanitation skills. With these skills, Orangi residents routinely maintain and repair their investments, lessening their dependence on OPP technical assistance.

---

18. "Orangi—A Model in Community Self-Help," *Inter Press Service*, 10/22/99.

19. "Mighty in Deed," *The Hindu*, 10/22/2000.

20. OPP itself was initially funded by BCCI and the United Nations Centre for Human Settlements (Habitat). Habitat refused to continue funding OPP after a few years, claiming that it was the idiosyncratic project of an individual, not an institutionalized project.

21. Namrita Talwar, "Cities without Slums," *UN Chronicle*, 3/1/2004.

Over the years, the OPP has identified and analyzed other problems in the Orangi area and developed additional programs, including:

- A basic health and family planning program which identifies the causes of common diseases in the area and the methods to preventing them, provides basic birth control and immunizations, and teaches about the importance of growing vegetables;

- A program to improve the housing construction industry in the area by introducing better machines to make cheaper concrete blocks and roof tiles, to upgrade the skills of local masons by introducing them to better construction techniques, and to educate house owners in planning and low-cost technology;

- A credit program for small family enterprises to improve production, employment opportunities, management skills, and business integrity;

- A program to upgrade the physical and educational conditions in schools established in the area by the private sector; and

- A program for women garment workers to build managerial skills and to organize so they can deal directly with wholesalers and exporters, eliminating exploitation by contractors and middlemen.[22]

---

22. UNESCAP, The Orangi Pilot Project, October 29, 2003.

3. Empowering Women

Over the past decade, significant research confirms what many have known for a long time: women are critical to economic development, building civil society, and stable democracy. If the goal is to improve health, nutrition or education, reduce fertility or child mortality, stem the spread of HIV, build robust and self-sustaining community organizations, increase per capita income, encourage grass-roots democracy, or reduce political extremism and violence, then focusing on women often provides more powerful results than any other intervention.

Fundamental change in women's empowerment and rights only occurs when there is *local and community ownership*. Progress typically occurs in private (for example, a father's decision to send his daughter to school). It is often informal and yet is very real (as opposed to symbolic). Change occurs family by family, village by village, and results in a transformation of values with respect to women and girls. Without local community ownership and support for women, government initiatives remain under attack and continue to struggle. It is true even in a country like Turkey after many years of lawmaking. Without community ownership, U.S. support for women's rights will remain vulnerable to accusations of secularism and Western cultural imperialism.

In this chapter we review some strategies that have been

demonstrated to work in promoting local and community ownership of educating girls and empowering women.

Women and
Development

The impact of gender disparities falls hardest on
women and girls, but ultimately all of society pays the cost.
Achieving gender equality is now recognized to be so central to
reducing poverty and improving governance that it has become
a development objective in its own right. The UN Millennium
Development Goals, the action plan agreed to unanimously by
all of the world's leaders in 2000 to attack global poverty, has
gender equality as one of its eight goals; and women's empowerment is widely viewed as critical for achieving *all* the Millennium Development Goals.[1]

Nobel Prize winning economist Amartya Sen has argued
that nothing is more important for development today than the
economic, political, and social participation of women.[2] Positively, an important sea-change is occurring with regard to
women in the developing world. In the past, development efforts
have focused on achieving for women a more equitable access
to resources—an important and much needed improvement to
women's well-being. Now, however, women are increasingly
seen not just as passive recipients of help, but instead as active
promoters of social transformations that can improve the lives
of an entire society. Progress in three areas in particular augurs

1. MDGs: i) Eradicate Poverty and Hunger ii) Achieve Universal Primary
Education iii) Promote Gender Equality and Empower Women iv) Reduce
Child Mortality v) Improve Maternal Health vi) Combat HIV/AIDS, Malaria
and Other Diseases vii) Ensure Environmental Stability viii) Develop a Global
Partnership for Development.

2. Amartya Sen, *Development As Freedom* (Anchor Books Edition, 2000),
189.

well for the increasingly active role that women can play as agents of change: increases in female education, control over resources, and political voice.

Girls' Education

While there is clearly no silver bullet for poverty reduction, many would argue that educating girls is *the* rocket booster of development. As an example, Lawrence Summers, as chief economist of the World Bank, concluded that investing in girls' education may be the highest return on investment that can be made in the developing world.[3] Educated women have fewer, healthier, and better educated children and generate more income than women with little or no schooling. Educating girls, therefore, creates a virtuous cycle for the community and the country.

Mounting empirical data indicate that the returns to educating girls are greater than the returns from educating boys.[4] The highest returns to schooling in low-income countries occur at the primary school level, and they tend to decline at secondary and higher educational levels. Since women in developing countries usually have lower levels of education than men, closing the gender gap in years of schooling generates higher returns than promoting educational investments that allow gender gaps to remain.

Educating girls also has substantial long-term benefits. Increasing a mother's schooling has a significantly larger positive impact on the next generation than does adding to a father's schooling by the same number of years. Empirical data, consis-

3. Lawrence H. Summers, "Investing in All the People," EDI Seminar Paper, No. 45, The World Bank, Washington, D.C., 1992.

4. *Engendering Development*, A World Bank Policy Research Report, 2001.

tent across many regions of the world, support this conclusion.[5] Educated mothers, more so than fathers, lead to better birth outcomes (e.g., higher birth weights and lower infant mortality), better child nutrition, lower child mortality, and earlier and more years of schooling for the children.

Girls' education also leads to lower fertility, which is important for countries trying to improve per capita income.[6] Better-educated women bear fewer children than less-educated women because they marry later and have fewer years of childbearing. They also know more about how to control fertility and have more confidence and ability to make decisions regarding reproduction. A three-year increase in the average education level of women is associated with as much as one fewer child per woman.[7] Studies from India now show that girls' education has a stronger correlation with declining fertility than family planning initiatives.[8]

Agricultural productivity is also positively impacted by female education. World Bank studies indicate that in areas where women have very low levels of education, providing women with at least one year of primary education can raise farm yields more than increasing land and fertilizer usage. Women tend to cultivate different crops than men, and they cannot rely on men to have and/or share relevant information for their farming needs. Moreover, women increasingly are responsible for managing the family farm as men seek non-farm employment. Their productivity depends more and more on their ability to access information. As the world experiences growing land constraints and

5. Ibid.

6. World Bank, World Bank Report, 1993.

7. Christopher Colclough with Keith M. Lewin, *Educating All the Children* (Oxford University Press, 1993).

8. National Family Health Survey, India, http://www.hetv.org/india/nfhs/research.html.

diminishing returns to fertilizer use, the next revolution in agricultural productivity may well be driven by educational gains for women.

The leverage of girls' education helps explain why regions of the world that have achieved the most economic and social progress in the last half-century—East Asia, Southeast Asia, and Latin America—are those that have most successfully closed their gender gaps in education. Conversely, regions that have lagged behind in their growth—notably South Asia, the Middle East, and sub-Saharan Africa—have lagged badly in their relative investments in girls' schooling, limiting women's contribution to economic and social progress. Adult female illiteracy today is highest in South Asia (55 percent), followed by the Arab world (51 percent), and Sub-Saharan Africa (45 percent). Simulation analyses suggest that had these three regions closed their gender gaps in education at the rate achieved by East Asia from 1960 to 1992, their income per capita could have grown by up to a full percentage point more per year than achieved. Compounded over three decades, that increase would have been significant.[9]

Control over Resources

Giving women more control over resources has also been shown to have positive benefits for the community. Simply put, women tend to invest more in the family than men. The benefits to the family of higher household income are greater if income is in the hands of the mother than the father. This enlarges the share of the household budget devoted to education, health, and nutrition-related expenditures, while decreasing the

9. http://www.undp.org/hdr2003/indicator/indic_216_1_1.html.

share spent on alcohol and cigarettes. This may seem clichéd, but the findings are consistent across a diverse set of countries, including Bangladesh, Brazil, Canada, the United Kingdom, and Ethiopia.[10]

The outcome is not trivial. For example, increases in female income improve child survival rates twenty times more than increases in male income. The marginal effect of female income for children's weight-height measures is about eight times as large. The same trends can be seen with respect to female borrowing versus male borrowing. Studies from Grameen Bank in Bangladesh show that female borrowing has a greater positive impact on children's school enrollments than does male borrowing.[11] It also has a large and statistically significant impact on children's nutrition and demand for healthcare, in contrast with male borrowing.

Women's empowerment may in fact be the most substantial impact of microfinance—the business of extending small loans to the poor with little or no collateral. Mohammed Yunus, who founded Bangladesh's Grameen Bank and launched the microfinance wave, reasoned that if loans were granted to poor people on appropriate and reasonable terms, "these millions of small people with their millions of small pursuits can add up to create the biggest development wonder."[12] Yunus has deliberately focused on women, for several reasons: women are the poorest of the poor, are more likely to be credit-constrained than men, have restricted access to the wage labor market, and have an inequitable share of power in household decision making. It has not hurt that the repayment rates of women microfinance clients

10. *Engendering Development*, A World Bank Policy Research Report, 2001.
11. Shahidur R. Khandker, *Fighting Poverty with Microcredit: Experience in Bangladesh*. Washington, D.C., World Bank, 1998.
12. Mohammed Yunus, Grameen Bank at a Glance, http://grameen-info .org/bank/.

are also superior to men's. Today, 80 percent of the world's nearly seventy million microfinance clients around the world are women.

Microfinance has been hailed for its poverty-alleviation and financial sustainability, but its greatest long-term impact could be in the way it changes the status of women in society. Women who receive microfinance loans experience increased involvement in family decision-making, participation in public action, mobility, and political and legal awareness. Several studies also show reduced domestic violence against female borrowers. Researchers speculate that this is a consequence of women being regarded as more valuable economic members of the family once they start generating income via their micro-credit loans.

Women, Democracy, and Extremism

In most failed societies and fragile states women are valued less than men. In Afghanistan under the Taliban, perhaps the most extreme case, women were brutally suppressed. Leading indicators of a low status for women include a large gender gap in literacy rates and a skewed gender ratio (ratio of males to females in the population). Societies with more boys than girls are indicative of inferior nutrition and healthcare for girls, and sex-selective abortion or infanticide.

Political scientist Steven Fish argues that when women are marginalized, it means fewer anti-authoritarian voices in politics, and an increased tendency for men to join fanatical religious and political brotherhoods. In the same vein, former Asia Foundation President William P. Fuller argues that the empowerment of women and girls in Bangladesh, which has occurred primarily through increased educational opportunities for girls, has been a major factor in limiting political and religious extremism there.

"There is no doubt that educated women limited the power of the mullahs," Fuller says.[13] Countries that constrain half of their populations have an impossible challenge of creating successful, prosperous states and can never achieve robust democracy.

Many of the countries that are having the greatest problems expanding opportunities for women and girls are Muslim-majority states. There is a tendency to view Islamic constraints on women as evidence of a deep culture clash between the West and conservative Muslim societies. The real culture clash, however, is more often within Muslim societies. Tensions over the role of women reflect the huge gaps that exist between highly traditional rural populations and their more modernized urban compatriots. The precise role of religion in traditional cultures is a subject of debate. Many people who work in Northwest Pakistan, for example, note that their real challenge is not Islam but tribal culture.[14] Tensions do, nevertheless, exist between religious fundamentalists and those who have a less rigid interpretation of Islam. These divisions are playing out to varying degrees from Nigeria to Indonesia, and they are markedly on display in the Middle East.

Modernization efforts in the Middle East have long been intertwined with changing the status of women. In Turkey, Ataturk had a strong commitment to drag his country into the modern era, in no small part by transforming the role of women in society. Ataturk had a strong belief in the intrinsic importance of women to society, and he launched many reforms to give women more equal rights and opportunities. After the abolition of the Ottoman Caliphate in 1924, he led the country on an

13. William P. Fuller, interview by A. Lawrence Chickering, September 9, 2005.

14. Carol Morris, who worked as a consultant for the British Council in the Northwest Frontier Province (NWFP) in Pakistan for many years, made this observation in an interview in 2001.

aggressive program of secularization. European constitutional law replaced *Sharia*, education became a monopoly of the state (religious schools were abolished), and traditional Muslim dress was prohibited. The new Civil Code abolished polygamy, and recognized the equal rights of women in divorce, custody, and inheritance. Segregation in education was ended, and women were given full political rights. A steady increase of women in the country's political life led to election of a female prime minister in Turkey in the mid-1990s.

Tunisian President Habib Bourguiba followed a similar authoritarian, top-down approach to women's empowerment as part of his broader modernization efforts after independence. In 1956, he adopted a revolutionary Code of Personal Status, which greatly enhanced women's rights. Polygamy was banned, a girls' consent for marriage was required, and the minimum marriage age was raised to seventeen. Women were also now allowed to sue for divorce. The Code was progressive not only for Tunisia, but for the world at that time. His actions stand in stark contrast to those of King Mohamed V in adjacent Morocco, which gained independence from France at the same time. Morocco adopted a highly restrictive personal status law—*moudawana*—which institutionalized many conservative constraints on women.

Tunisia and Morocco's different attitudes toward women have produced significantly different results in human capital development. Overall literacy is 70 percent in Tunisia, (80 percent for men and 60 percent for women), versus only 48 percent in Morocco (60 percent for men and 35 percent for women).[15] Tunisia's better-educated workforce has been a major factor in making Tunisia a more attractive destination for foreign direct

15. http://stats.unctad.org/fdi/eng/ReportFolders/Rfview/Explorerp.asp?C S_referer=.

investment. Today, tens of thousands of women in Tunisia have earned a ticket to the middle class for their families by working in export-oriented light manufacturing and foreign service-centers. Not surprisingly, Tunisia's population growth rate is also notably lower than Morocco's, which has allowed it to achieve stronger gains in per capita income. Tunisian women on average have 2.3 children (near replacement level) versus 3.4 children per woman in Morocco today.

The top-down authoritarian approach of Ataturk and Bourguiba to women's rights has not been without significant backlash. The concept of female empowerment has come to be linked strongly with notions of secularism and Western cultural imperialism, generating widespread resistance from both men and women. Faced with strong pressure from religious conservatives, leaders throughout the region have appeased fundamentalists by giving them significant, continuing influence over the role of women in society—usually through personal status codes and family law that are defining for women. Today, with the importance of women to economic and political development becoming increasingly clear and imperative, several reformist leaders—like King Mohamed VI in Morocco, King Abdullah in Jordan, and Sheik Hamad in Qatar—are beginning to reassess that bargain. All young (Mohamed and Abdullah are in their early forties, and Hamad is in his mid-fifties) and Western-educated, they are engaged—working with their wives, Princess Lalla Salma in Morocco, Queen Rania in Jordan, and Sheika Mouza in Qatar—in a delicate balancing act of pushing women forward without alienating their still highly conservative societies. Their ability to succeed has wide repercussions not only for their countries, but also for the region and the world.

Tiny Qatar, a highly conservative Wahhabi state, provides perhaps the most startling example of change. Sheik Hamad has launched a number of political reforms, including holding the country's first popular election in 1999. Men and women were allowed to vote and run for office. He and his wife, Sheika Mouza, have also promoted education reform. The Rand Corporation has been hired to advise on restructuring the country's educational system. Meanwhile, the government-backed Education City initiative is expanding. It has already attracted several American universities to set up local branches, including a Virginia Commonwealth School of Arts and a Weill Cornell Medical College. Sheika Mouza has been a driving force behind these efforts and has ensured that women play a prominent role. Women now make up more than 60 percent of university graduates in the country. Although Qatar's population is less than a million (with approximately 200,000 citizens), its example, particularly with regard to women, ripples significantly beyond its borders. The question remains, however, what influence it wields given its size and the fact that it has no substantial traditional, rural culture, as the other countries do.

Saudi Arabia today presents one of the greatest foreign policy challenges for the United States. Most of the terrorists who took over the planes on 9/11 were Saudi, and Saudi resources continue to fuel extremist thought throughout the region and around the world. Saudi Arabia today also remains extremely conservative in its attitude toward women, with some of the most restrictive laws to be found anywhere regarding women's role in society. Religious conservatives maintain strict control over women's access to public life. Segregation of society is nearly complete—in health care, education, and the work force. Women are treated as minors: they must have a male guardian in public, they are not allowed to drive, and they must have permission from their closest male relative to travel. The notorious mutaween—religious police—patrol the malls to ensure that women are fully covered in public.[16] Women were denied

16. In a tragic incident in 2002, fifteen school girls in Mecca were killed

the vote in Saudi Arabia's municipal elections, held in February 2005. With women granted the vote in neighboring Kuwait in 2005, Saudi Arabia is the only country in the Middle East to deny women the right to participate in elections. In a recent Freedom House survey of women's rights in the Middle East, Saudi Arabia scored the lowest of the seventeen countries.[17]

Saudi oil wealth has enabled the promotion of its highly conservative form of Islam—and notions of women—throughout the world, with notable impact over the past twenty five years in Nigeria, Pakistan, and Indonesia. But pressure for change is brewing within the kingdom. Female literacy in Saudi Arabia has risen from 2 percent in the mid-1960s, when universal female education was introduced, to more than 70 percent today. Now, women constitute nearly 60 percent of all university students. Today's far more educated generation of women is beginning to question the constraints on their lives. Women's rights have become a theme intertwined with the demand for increased human rights. Economic circumstances have also fueled the pressure for change. With per capita income down by half today, more Saudis are questioning the practice of handicapping half the country's human capital. Recent high oil prices have provided some economic relief to the kingdom, but not enough to raise per capita GNP significantly, given the country's rapid population growth rate.[18]

Today, local newspapers are filled with discussions over the role of women in Saudi society. Even the controversial ban on women driving is being raised publicly again. The debate over

---

in a fire. The mutaween were accused of forcing the girls back inside the burning building because they were not appropriately covered.

17. Freedom House. "Citizenship and Justice: A Survey of Women's Rights in the Middle East and North Africa," April 2005.

18. "Saudi Arabia." *Encyclopaedia Britannica*. 2005. Encyclopaedia Britannica Premium Service 13 July 2005, http://www.britannica.com/eb/article?toc Id=6434.

women's rights in the kingdom can be seen as a proxy for the more difficult and dangerous debate over human rights, civil liberties, and religious extremism that is percolating in the country. Indeed, pressures to empower women are being felt throughout the Muslim world. Resistance, however, remains strong within traditional cultures and especially in rural areas. This continuing resistance highlights an important lesson for countries, including the U.S., committed to promoting women's rights. History shows that women's empowerment only happens in sustainable fashion when communities accept and ultimately embrace the changes.

Two Challenges in Promoting Women's Rights

The reason that women's empowerment continues to be so difficult in parts of the world, even in countries like Tunisia and Turkey which have long histories of promoting women's rights, is that change requires both top-down leadership and bottom-up support.

Top-down leadership usually results in public, legal, and often highly symbolic changes. It has to do with creating constitutions and passing laws guaranteeing women's rights. This is the part that governments need to do. It is the part that progressive governments around the world have been doing, and the U.S. has been supporting in a variety of ways. This part depends on local ownership by political elites who—to a large extent—share cosmopolitan values. But even if rights command powerful followings among urban elites in developing countries, few people living in traditional villages in the countryside support any broad concept of individual rights, and governments cannot compel compliance. Therefore, promoting the *reality* of women's empowerment—beyond formal, legal rights—requires support from another source. That is the second part of the challenge.

The only effective way to achieve women's empowerment and rights—changing traditional, rural cultures—is through community ownership and community-based initiatives. To promote women's rights without continuing resistance, governments need to move beyond state initiatives and develop civil society initiatives. Fortunately, there are many powerful examples showing how to do this. One of these can be found around the city of Asyut in Upper Egypt, the "epicenter of Islamic terrorism" in Egypt. Others can be found in the deeply conservative tribal areas of northern Pakistan and in rural Afghanistan.

Case Studies from Upper Egypt, Northern Pakistan, and Afghanistan

In Egypt's urban areas—as in many developing countries—one is as likely to find girls in school as boys. But the picture is starkly different in rural areas—again, as in many developing countries. In Egypt's southern, rural region, huge disparities exist between male and female enrollment in schools. To meet this challenge, UNICEF, with the strong collaboration of Egypt's Ministry of Education, established a Community Schools Initiative (CSI) in 1992 in the governorates of Asyut, Sohag, and Qena. The idea was to encourage female education in Egypt's rural context, which meant overcoming the obstacles associated with girls' education in a highly conservative, poverty stricken environment.

From the very start, the CSI relied on heavy participation of communities to promote a sense of community ownership of the schools, which (it was believed) would help make even the most traditional parents comfortable with the idea of educating their girls. The teachers, or facilitators, in the classroom were selected in close consultation with the community and were trained to encourage, guide, and evaluate the students. Students, in turn, were given the skills to think critically and participate actively in the classroom. With a heavy emphasis on peer learning, the "system [was] designed to foster a real sense of democracy and community," explains Malak Zaalouk, education officer at UNICEF and founder of the program, "and this shows in the changing behavior of the children. They become more independent and speak confidently in front of the class."

Since its inception, UNICEF's Community Schools Project has established more than 200 schools, with 6,500 students, 70 percent of them girls. The average rate of graduates going on to preparatory school is more than 90 percent. Perhaps most interestingly, the schools have promoted significant changes in community attitudes toward girls and women. Many of the fathers who before the schools would not let their girls out of their homes will now let them go to Cairo to college.

The Egyptian Ministry of Education has been a key player in the success of the Community Schools Initiative. It provides teacher salaries, textbooks, and administers tests to ensure that CSI students are able effectively to integrate into the secondary school system. The Community Schools Project has inspired the government-sponsored Mubarak One Classroom initiative, which has used the same models of learning employed in the schools of Upper Egypt. Other donors, such as CIDA and USAID, have stepped in and replicated the effort in other rural areas of Egypt. The aim of donors is to provide sustained financial support to these schools until community organizations, non-government partners, and the Ministry of Education are able to integrate the schools into the government's One Classroom Initiative. The impact of the Community Schools Initiative has been enormously positive. Girls, in otherwise hard-to-reach areas, are provided with a basic education, instilling in them a sense of confidence and pride, and benefiting the whole community. Perhaps the greatest impact of community schools is their ability to alter the culture of traditional villages and their attitudes towards women.

The work of American activist Greg Mortenson also highlights the importance of community ownership. Since the mid-1990s, Mortenson has founded forty-eight girls' schools in the northern territories in Pakistan, a bastion of fundamentalist, tribal Islam. He provides a powerful example of what is possible even under the most difficult circumstances. In addition to the schools he has founded in Pakistan, he is working with an alliance of forty tribal leaders in northern Afghanistan, who have come together in part through their common support of educating girls.[19] Mortenson insists that when donor-funded projects fail, it is often due to a lack of community ownership. He relates stories about new, donor-funded schools in Afghanistan, with crisp new Afghan flags flying high, but not a child in sight, while down the road hundreds of Afghan children are huddled under ancient UNICEF tents. Why are the new schools empty and unused? He says it is because the community—tribal elders, parents, religious leaders—did not participate in the process of creating the schools and therefore remain suspicious of them.

Other powerful examples can be found in what might seem the most difficult of places to pursue female empowerment: Afghanistan. The non-profit group Future Generations has achieved significant success working with religious and tribal leaders throughout central Afghanistan to build support for girls' education. Not willing to wait until a school building is con-

19. He has had two *fatwahs* issued against him but has had both formally countermanded—the first by the Grand Council of Ayatollahs in Teheran, declaring the education of girls an important imperative of Islam; and the second by a similar body in Islamabad.

structed, many remote villages have begun using their local mosque—the only existing communal building in the area—to educate both the boys and girls. Future Generations has enlisted the support of the local mullahs to endorse education for both girls and boys, and to provide the mosque for girls' literacy classes on those days it is not being used for religious services.

Another innovative program that is beginning to change the role of women within Afghanistan's highly conservative society is the National Solidarity Program (NSP), an internationally funded effort to organize community elections. Elders have traditionally ruled Afghan villages, but now a new class of leaders, elected by the community, is emerging. Early indications are that women are playing an important role in this development. In the first 352 villages that held NSP-supported elections (across five provinces), 76 percent of eligible women voted compared with 69 percent of eligible men. These voters elected 2,289 women and 3,755 men to their local councils. The profile of those elected is typically under thirty-five, more literate, but generally poorer than average in the community. This is a profound change for Afghanistan, where age and wealth have been the defining factors for village leadership for centuries. By May 2005 the NSP had rolled out its community mobilization program to 8,268 villages, of which 7,348 had elected Community Development Councils. The program is under implementation in 159 districts in thirty-three of Afghanistan's thirty-four provinces.[20]

The goal of the NSP is to stimulate community mobilization and local ownership of development. It also provides a mechanism to deliver services such as literacy and health. Donors, including USAID, have committed $170 million through the Min-

20. http://www.worldbank.org.af/WBSITE/EXTERNAL/COUNTRIES/ SOUTHASIAEXT/AFGHANISTANEXTN/0,,contentMDK:20565783~me nuPK:305990~pagePK:141137~piPK:141127~theSitePK:305985,00.html.

istry of Rehabilitation and Rural Development for community block grants, which vary between $5,000 and $60,000 depending on the size of the community. The village must submit a proposal and use the funds within one year. Elected leaders have received training in financial accounting, management, and conflict resolution.

If women continue to participate in this emerging grassroots democracy as they have done in the early stages, this will indeed be a revolutionary development. The advances that women have made over the past hundred years in Afghanistan have been almost wholly confined to urban areas, touching only a very small portion of the population. If women at the local level can begin to play a significant role in public life and resource allocation, that will represent long and lasting change, and forms the basis for important economic development.

These are only a few of many examples where community ownership of girls' education and women's empowerment can be found even in the most challenging, fundamentalist regions of Upper Egypt, Northwest Pakistan, and Afghanistan. These programs demonstrate how community attitudes towards women and girls can be shifted within a relatively short timeframe (a few years) even in the most traditional, rural areas.

Implications
for U.S. Policy

The Bush administration recognizes the importance of women to the development of societies. In fact, the promotion of women's rights has been a prominent element of its nation-building efforts in both Afghanistan and Iraq, and a central motif of its efforts to promote democracy in the Middle East. However, an enormous, apparent dilemma has obstructed the administration's commitment. It wants to promote democracy and rights, but without destabilizing authoritarian regimes that are supporting its war on terrorism.

Commitment to civil society initiatives may hold an answer to this dilemma. In Afghanistan, U.S. policymakers were instrumental in pushing for women's rights in the country's new constitution. Debate over the role of women during constitutional negotiations revealed deep fault lines in society. U.S. influence was widely acknowledged as a moderating factor and critical in securing for women a 25 percent electoral quota in parliament. This step, while potentially significant, runs the risk of being merely symbolic if not sustained by strong civil society initiatives to build community support for broad-based women's empowerment.

For Afghan women to take advantage of their new economic and political opportunities, they must greatly enhance their education. Female literacy—as defined by being able to read a newspaper and write a letter—is well below 20 percent in Afghanistan. Girls' education is a stated priority for USAID, and now more girls are attending school in Afghanistan than ever before in the nation's history. USAID's commitment to education in Afghanistan is $100 million over the next two years. Since the challenge there is not only reforming education for the next generation, but also creating opportunities for older girls and women, a Country Strategic Plan for Afghanistan could well decide that $100 million is grossly insufficient, especially since the bulk of that funding is devoted to school construction. Only a small portion is directed to meeting girls' most pressing educational need: the training of female teachers.

The gains women have achieved in Afghanistan over the past two years are tenuous at best. Several of the powerful warlords in de facto control of large swaths of the country are not fans of women's rights. Their militias have burned down girls' schools, and some of them pressured village leaders not to allow women to vote in the presidential elections held in September, 2004. The U.S. continues to provide these leaders with tacit and explicit support to gain their cooperation in the hunt for terrorists. Turkey's experience after eighty years suggests that it may take much longer than a generation and strong international support for women to achieve a substantive improvement in their status in Afghanistan—*unless* it implements strong civil society initiatives to promote girls' education. Greg Mortenson's experience in northern Afghanistan probably holds some important lessons on how to be successful in promoting community support there.

While it may seem obvious why both progressive and authoritarian Muslim governments are experiencing resistance to women's rights, community-based initiatives can play an important role in reducing the resistance. Without a genuine effort to achieve ownership by traditional, rural cultures, governments are right to fear chaos on the one side and Islamic fundamentalism on the other. However, with strong community-based initiatives promoting girls' education and women's empowerment, societies can begin to move toward democracy and rights while potentially avoiding both chaos and religious extremism.

In dealing with reluctant governments, special priority should be given to decentralized, civil society initiatives, which can demonstrate how even the most traditional, rural parts of a society can be encouraged to support women's empowerment.

Developing a Civil Society Strategy

The best way to design a civil society initiative for women's empowerment is to examine programs that have actually worked. There are ample examples of deeply conservative, traditional communities which have embraced girls' education.

The key to success is to work with community leaders from the beginning. When the initiatives come from local communities themselves, facilitated by local CSOs, they become homegrown experiments in popular democracy.

Ultimately, achieving large-scale increases in girls' enrollments depends on reforming government schools, which serve the great majority of children. If community ownership is the key to getting girls in school, then community ownership needs to be achieved in government schools, which are often bureaucratic, mechanical, and unfriendly to parents. This is a challenge that deserves substantial investment in research and development. Educate Girls Globally (EGG) may have found at least part of the answer. Working with a local partner in northern India, EGG has developed a strategy for mobilizing local communities, working with teachers, to "take ownership" of government schools and make them work for girls. EGG has tested the strategy in more than 1,000 schools. Because the government continues to finance all principal costs of running the schools and EGG's only costs are for facilitation and training, the process is extremely inexpensive. It also has the potential of working at very high scales. Finally, it is showing an unusual potential to gain government support.[21]

In promoting women's empowerment to central governments, arguments that emphasize economic benefits have special power. By focusing on the compelling economic rationale for

---

21. In a recent evaluation of the program completed by the International Center for Research on Women (ICRW), on a grant from the Ford Foundation, the evaluators affirmed that although a great deal of additional experimentation and evaluation is needed, the process shows considerable promise and potential for effecting a variety of changes of attitude in traditional communities that could be important for educating girls and empowering adult women. Upala Banerjee, "From Research to Action: Evaluating a Rights-based, Demand Driven Model for Improving Girls' Education in the Government Schools of Tehri Garhwal, Uttaranchal," June 2005.

women's empowerment, the U.S. can find common ground with local actors striving to improve living standards for all.

As the experience in Afghanistan shows, U.S. efforts to advance women's rights—particularly in Muslim societies—is a complicated and delicate task. Different strategies are obviously necessary for different countries. Respect for women's rights should become a more explicit component of conditionality for U.S. military and economic aid. The State Department could begin publicly reporting on countries' progress on key gender measures such as girls' literacy, maternal health, gender ratios, and political participation, much as it does on human rights. While these actions will help encourage change on the part of governments, a strong commitment to civil society initiatives, building community support for empowering women and girls, may be the most powerful action in producing real change.

As we stated in the first chapter, we believe foreign assistance should be guided by country plans that identify key strategies and results to achieve positive change, especially in priority states. Country strategists should give strong priority to initiatives that improve the status of women, especially in the Middle East, South Asia, and Sub-Saharan Africa, where gender gaps are largest. Because of the demonstrated high returns on investment in girls' education, the U.S. should make the elimination of gender gaps in basic and primary education its top development priority. USAID support for basic education today is less than $250 million, and very little of it is allocated specifically to girls.

Expanding girls' education will encourage girls to postpone marriage, which will in turn reduce fertility while also helping reduce infant and maternal mortality rates. Women's health and family planning, particularly in areas like Afghanistan with dire statistics, also deserve increased funding because adequate primary, maternal, and reproductive healthcare are critical for women's empowerment. This is particularly true in countries with high rates of adolescent marriage. The Middle East Partnership Initiative, the $150 million program administered by the State Department to promote democracy in the Middle East, has a number of initiatives focused on women, including female literacy and health, and business and political training. USAID and the state should ensure that its efforts are well coordinated to maximize strategic impact. Such initiatives should be implemented through CSOs to promote community ownership, along with attention to development of education systems that give special priority to girls and women.

As the U.S. undertakes the largest expansion of foreign development aid in more than a generation through the Millennium Challenge Account (MCA), specific gender measures should be incorporated into the eligibility criteria. None of the sixteen criteria currently proposed for determining eligibility provide a direct measure of women's status or gender equality. Yet several measures exist that provide a reasonable indication of gender equality and also correlate strongly with development outcomes (examples are the maternal mortality ratio and the female primary school completion rate). Including these would undoubtedly improve the effectiveness of the MCA. Most importantly, these initiatives need to be implemented through strong involvement of civil society organizations as well as government agencies, as possible.

Finally, the U.S. should be leading the world on implementing UN Resolution 1325, passed unanimously by the General Assembly in 2000, in which the UN commits to making women more central to peacekeeping efforts and post-conflict transitions. This is a crucial part of recruiting citizens as partners in reducing conflict and promoting peace, which we discuss in the next chapter. While the U.S. has been supportive of Resolution 1325, women need to play a major role in such citizen initiatives.

Conclusion

Since the attacks of September 11, a concerted effort has been underway to identify and address the causes of political and economic stagnation in the Middle East. In 2002, the UN published the groundbreaking Arab Human Development Report, written by Arab economists and intellectuals. The report attributed the region's lack of democracy to three factors: the freedom deficit, the knowledge deficit, and a lack of women's empowerment. The authors argued that unless women are allowed to realize their economic, intellectual, and leadership potential, liberalization attempts in these countries will continue to founder.

We have noted that the role of women continues to be a political and social flashpoint in many conservative societies. In particular, women's rights represent the frontline battlefield between religious extremists and those with a more modern, progressive vision. The battle is playing out vividly today in countries like Saudi Arabia and Afghanistan, and to a lesser extent in many other countries from Nigeria to Egypt to Pakistan to Indonesia. The outcome is critical: those countries that limit the role of women in society—systematically limiting their educational opportunities, control over resources, and economic and political participation—will stagnate economically and be unable to develop democratic institutions.

With the strategic value of women's empowerment in the region now well established, the U.S. government has been vocal about including women in its various democratization programs in the Middle East. But although the administration gets an "A" for rhetoric, its promotion of women's rights has been inconsistent. The U.S. has linked calls for democracy with increased rights for women, but it has supported a women's empowerment agenda in reform-oriented countries (Morocco), while holding back in countries where the government is less amenable (Saudi Arabia). The experience with community elections in Afghanistan suggests that a powerful, community-based approach to empowering women politically will work. The U.S. needs to accelerate this program there, and it also needs to do more for women economically.

One of our conclusions here is part of an overall conclusion of this essay: that the U.S. is not funding civil society initiatives in different areas of economic and political need at nearly the levels of their strategic value. We believe this is certainly true for programs designed to raise the status of women. The issue of strategic value needs to be examined across all of the issues considered in this essay, and ultimately it also should be considered as the "guiding standard" for the preparation of Country Strategic Plans. In the case of women's empowerment and rights, we have discussed some of their major components having to do with educating girls and empowering women economically and politically. Other components include maternal parent education and child development, maternal health and family planning, microfinance, and women's political training. All of these components should be considered in developing strategic initiatives supporting women.

As former Secretary of State Colin Powell said, "the worldwide advancement of women's issues is not only in keeping with the deeply held values of the American people; it is strongly in our national interest as well." Economic data overwhelmingly show that women are critical to development, and more evidence is emerging that expanding the role of women in society helps promote good governance and stable societies. It is time the U.S. better aligned its policies to reflect the centrality of women's rights and women's empowerment to its strategic interests. To accomplish this, the U.S. needs to commit to a strategy that includes a major role for civil society.

4. Citizens as Partners in the Search for Peace

In early 2005 the death of Yasir Arafat, the election of Mahmoud Abbas, and the willingness of the government of Israel to withdraw from Gaza combined to raise hopes that a new peace process might be possible in the Middle East. The election of Abbas was part of the peace initiative that George Bush and Tony Blair committed themselves to the previous November— a two-state solution to the Israeli-Palestinian conflict. The ambition at the time was to end terrorism, hold elections, and assemble international support for Palestinian development.

The optimism may yet prove prophetic. But unless the new process takes Israeli and Palestinian societies into account—including the role that religion plays in them—the new round of peacemaking will very likely meet the same obstacles that blocked past initiatives for peace. In that event, this latest effort will collapse in violence, damaging the security interests of Israel, the Palestinians, friendly governments in the region, and the United States. But even if the process succeeds in creating a fragile peace between Israelis and Palestinians, other peace proposals in the Middle East ultimately failed because they were not supplemented by programs aimed at reforming societies and building a culture of peace in them.

For decades the parties to the peace process have concentrated on state-to-state relations without considering how societies, both Israeli and Palestinian, constrain state power. Palestinians who seemed too eager to make peace with Israel have repeatedly found themselves pushed aside and even killed by their compatriots. Intolerance toward Israel permeates life in the occupied territories, from school lessons to official speeches. Peace treaties have been signed between Israel, Egypt, and Jordan, but even these agreements remain fragile because of societal opposition to normal relations.

However cordial government relations may be, it would be hard to argue that any of the signs of normality characterize relations between Israel and Egypt. It is a "cold peace." There is little spontaneous exchange, certainly no deep and sustained mutual engagement across the two societies. And the architect of the peace, Anwar Sadat, was assassinated not long after his visit to Jerusalem. A similar societal estrangement exists between Jordan and Israel.

Israeli society has proved just as unyielding. As Labor Prime Minister Ehud Barak approached the climax of peacemaking during the Clinton administration, he lost his parliamentary majority. Yitzhak Rabin was assassinated by a Jewish extremist for his seeming willingness to return most of the occupied territories, and Ariel Sharon has received death threats because of his commitment to evacuate Gaza.

The Palestinians are as divided as Israelis about peace, with those in favor constantly exposed to overbidding by Islamic terrorists and the older generation of Arafat supporters. In such circumstances, it is no wonder peace talks fly apart with bitter recriminations from all sides.

We introduce the subject of this chapter—recruiting citizens as partners in the search for peace—by pointing to the Middle East not because we claim that society-based initiatives can, by themselves, bring peace. Formal state-to-state negotiations are necessary to accomplish that. We only argue that such informal, non-state initiatives—including initiatives aimed at religious leaders—supporting and supplementing the formal process will greatly increase the chances of success. This is true not only in achieving an agreement, but also in sustaining both the letter and spirit of it. Moreover, if the current Palestinian-Israeli peace initiative fails, we urge that the U.S. government make a commitment to a society-based initiative, which will help prepare the ground for new formal negotiations when the parties are ready to commit to them.[1]

In this chapter we consider the role that informal society-based initiatives have played in various conflicts—in India, Northern Ireland, South Africa, and Burundi. We start in India because it reveals the model for reducing conflicts—there between Hindus and Muslims. We then look at Northern Ireland because informal initiatives played such an important role over a number of years in supporting the formal peace negotiations that ultimately led to a reasonably stable agreement in 1998 and have continued to limit conflict to tolerable levels there. We also look at South Africa and at Burundi because they present some interesting case studies of conflict reduction under difficult conditions.

1. Some people argue that although a society-based initiative could have been hugely effective after Oslo, such an initiative would not be effective in the current atmosphere. They go on to say that it would be virtually impossible to put together now and would be greeted on both sides as "been there, done that." The first answer is contained in the objection: since it was *not* done before, there is no problem of "been there, done that." This objection comes from people in the peace movement who have been trying to do this but on a very limited scale and have never been supported by any official peace process. If the entire terms of the peace process were changed, and commitment to a society-based initiative made an explicit requirement of the process, one can imagine that its prospects for success would be very different. It is certainly not impossible to do; there are lots of activities underway that are trying to do this—for instance, by groups like the Israel-Palestine Center for Research and Information. They just need to be substantially expanded and recognized by the official peace process.

This chapter focuses on a variety of models for reducing conflict. These are essential, but it is important to appreciate that they are not the only society-based initiatives that can make a difference in helping promote peace in a place like the Middle East. We will mention others.

Hindu-Muslim
Conflict in India

In his book *Ethnic Conflict and Civic Life*, Ahutosh Varshney studies religious conflict in India between Hindus and Muslims and addresses the question of why, despite religious diversity, some communities managed to maintain relative peace over long periods of time while others erupted periodically into violence. The study is based on all reported Hindu-Muslim riots in India between 1950 and 1995.

Here is Varshney's conclusion about the most important reason Hindus and Muslims were able to avoid major outbreaks of violence:

> [T]he pre-existing local networks of civic engagement between the two communities [Hindu and Muslim] stand out as the single most important *proximate* causes. Where such networks of engagements exist, tensions and conflicts were regulated and managed; where they are missing, communal identities led to endemic and ghastly violence.[2]

The author distinguishes two kinds of civic networks: *associational* forms of engagement and *everyday* forms. Associational forms of engagement are institutional: business organizations, professional associations, trade unions, reading clubs, and sports clubs. Everyday forms involve simple, everyday forms of inter-

2. Ahutosh Varshney, *Ethnic Conflict and Civic Life: Hindus and Muslims in India*, 2nd ed. (New Haven: Yale University Press, 2002), 9.

action: socializing informally, children playing together. While both can play a valuable role in promoting peace, Varshney finds that the associational forms of engagement are more powerful and enduring in promoting peace than the everyday forms.

The conclusion that civic engagement is the most important factor containing religious conflict raises an interesting paradox: there are far more formal mechanisms for civic engagement in cities than in the countryside; yet most communal violence takes place in cities. The author concludes that although rural areas have few formal institutions of engagement, the enormous number of ways to engage informally build and sustain trust in "village-like intimacy," and these in turn promote peace. The apparent contradiction (the author's claim that formal engagement is more powerful but that informal engagement in rural areas brings more peace) is resolved by the intensity and scale of (weaker) engagement in the countryside.

Varshney describes the importance of informal associations as follows:

> Routine engagement allows people to come together and form temporary organizations in times of tension. Such organizations, though short-run, turned out to be highly significant. Called peace committees and consisting of members of both communities, these organizations policed neighbourhoods, killed rumors, provided information to the local administration, and facilitated communication between communities in times of tension.[3]

This study serves as a valuable introduction to the subject of conflict reduction because it highlights so clearly the model, based on personal face-to-face engagement, that is effective in reducing violence.

Vershney's study of India provides an interesting introduc-

3. Ibid., 9–10.

tion to consider these issues in relation to Northern Ireland. In his conclusion he comments on Northern Ireland by citing a study by John Darby of variances in violence in three local communities in Greater Belfast: Kileen-Banduff, the Upper Ashbourne Estates, and Dunville.[4] While all three communities have mixed Catholic and Protestant populations, the first two experienced considerable violence since the late 1960s, while the third has not. While all three had segregated churches, schools and political parties, Darby found that Dunville had mixed Rotary and Lions Clubs and mixed sports clubs (soccer, bowling, cricket, boxing, etc.)—as well as a vibrant, mixed Single Parents Club.

The overall lesson is that when *personal engagement* is missing, habitual tribal and religious loyalties are vulnerable to passionate antagonism and even hatred of "other"—leading to terrible violence, in India, Northern Ireland, and other places. With personal engagement, however, comes trust and connection—engagement of others as human. This can only happen in intimate spaces, although—as we shall see in the case of Burundi below—it can be greatly strengthened by the use of media.

Understanding why civic engagement played such a central role in reducing conflict between Hindus and Muslims in India brings into play the same factors, we believe, that explain why civic engagement played such an important role in supporting the formal negotiations in Northern Ireland. In India, of course, there was no national peace-keeping effort: informal accommodation and peace-making had to operate village-by-village.

4. John Darby, *Intimidation and the Control of Conflict in Northern Ireland* (Dublin: Gill and MacMillan, 1986).

Northern
Ireland

Brandeis political scientist Mari Fitzduff begins her discussion of informal, Track Two, diplomacy in Northern Ireland by emphasizing the silence in private conversations between people in Northern Ireland and the difficulties promoting dialogue between them.[5] Personal dialogue between politicians and paramilitaries on opposing sides, she notes, is even more difficult because they are closely watched by their communities. At various times conventions have dictated whom one is "permitted" to speak to.[6]

These circumstances created substantial impediments both to informal dialogue and mediation and to formal negotiations in Northern Ireland. Ignorance and distrust between the political parties retarded formal negotiations (Track One initiatives), and the very public nature of such negotiations limited their effectiveness in building trust and in achieving dialogue that included all relevant parties. This was especially true of the groups that had not renounced violence: the paramilitaries and political parties thought to be aligned with paramilitaries.

Informal (Track Two) initiatives[7] are more flexible and private but often lack resources and standing to translate successful dialogues into formal agreements. But both formal (Track One)

5. This discussion relies substantially on Mari Fitzduff, "Provoking Dialogue—the Northern Ireland Experience," in *Peacebuilding: A Field Guide*, eds. Luc Reychler and Thana Pffenholz (Bolder, CO: Lynne Rienner Publishers, 2001).

6. Unionists have at times refused to talk to all other non-unionist parties and the British government; the SDLP has refused to talk formally with others in the Assembly (1982–86); and churches, government ministers and others have usually refused to talk to Sinn Fein for most of the conflict.

7. The phrase "Track Two" was introduced by William D. Davidson and Joseph Montville twenty-five years ago in an article called "Foreign Policy According to Freud," which was published in *Foreign Affairs* in 1981.

and informal (Track Two) initiatives played important, complementary roles in the eventual success of the peace process in Northern Ireland.

Over the twenty-five years of formal, Track One initiatives, from the early 1970s until the agreement was finally signed on April 10, 1998—the so-called "Good Friday Agreement"—negotiations gradually expanded participation so that by the final stage of negotiations all major stakeholders were included. In the beginning, for more than twenty years, formal negotiations were held only with parties willing to renounce violence in furtherance of their objectives. Over time, space was found to include paramilitaries who refused to renounce violence. The most important of these was Sinn Fein, which is the political movement that seeks the merger of Northern Ireland into Ireland.

In the beginning the British could see no value in having the Irish government formally participate in the negotiations, but in 1985 the British signed an agreement bringing in the Irish government. The final negotiations included a wide range of participants, including the paramilitaries.

A variety of informal, Track Two mediation initiatives made significant contributions to the formal negotiations. Among the most important Track Two participants were community mediators, academics, churches, business and citizen mediators from the United States. Women also played a significant role in many Track Two initiatives. In general, these efforts concentrated on developing productive contacts between politicians, between the paramilitaries and governments, and between politicians and civil society.

The most significant efforts were probably the many hundreds of initiatives throughout the conflict facilitating contact or communications between disputants. Most of these contacts were facilitated by local mediators, but they were supported by mediators from abroad, especially Quakers. These programs sought to create safe spaces for politicians to consider issues of common interest apart from the conflict. Various initiatives looked at problems including social issues, the economy, and conflicts elsewhere. The initiatives' principal purpose was to build trust. These initiatives generally avoided issues related to the conflict because of the belief these should be left to formal negotiations.

In addition, thousands of people were involved in community initiatives promoting dialogue between communities, and in the early 1990s, these dialogues increased significantly. Many organizations sponsored training programs for these dialogues, and there were hundreds of local workshops that brought together people from all sectors of the community to discuss a wide variety of issues, with political options, for their future together. Other initiatives aimed to stimulate dialogue through other media, including drama, music, and art programs.

It is interesting that in the years preceding the agreement a large increase in cross-community attendance appeared at the funerals of victims of political and sectarian assassinations, as trade unionist and other groups sponsored huge public demonstrations against continuing violence. Initiatives such as these made important contributions in developing an environment in the community ready for a political agreement.

Although most academics remained aloof from the conflict, some made important contributions to constructive dialogue. One example was the development of a Northern Ireland Centre in Brussels in the early 1990s, created by academics at the University of Ulster. The Centre was established under the auspices of both the political parties and the business community, and it helped foster knowledge and trust between them. During the 1990s academics also helped organize workshops for politicians and others to meet outside the country to address issues related to the conflict and its resolution. Holding the meetings in other countries provided opportunities for people to form relationships that were difficult to form at home.

In 1992 an independent citizen's group called Initiative 92 put out a general request from both institutions and individuals to propose ideas about possible strategies for economic, political, and social progress in Northern Ireland. Although condemned by politicians, who were threatened by it, the initiative was extremely successful in engaging public participation in the search for peace. More than five hundred proposals came forward from people and groups in the country, and more importantly, many of them were developed by different communities working together and cooperating.

Initiative 92 made every citizen an active stakeholder in searching for ways forward. One feature of the initiative was sponsorship of public workshops that allowed people and groups proposing ideas to expand on them in public fora. Thus, for each idea other people and groups had opportunities to come forward and co-create the proposals. This greatly expanded "ownership" of the proposals. In 1993 these proposals were published in an enormous book for Northern Ireland called *The Opsahl Report*. Many of these proposals played an important role in eventually facilitating the final agreement.

Since the conflict had powerful religious underpinnings, the churches contributed very little to Track Two dialogues and contacts, but there were some exceptions. Some members of the Catholic clergy played a role in initiating and expanding dialogue with Sinn Fein, and they also sponsored private, off-the-record workshops for several years in the mid-1990s between Sinn Fein and members of the Protestant/Unionist clergy.

Although many in the Unionist community expressed great hostility to these dialogues between Sinn Fein and Unionist clergy when they were eventually revealed, the meetings nevertheless created a valuable space within which Sinn Fein could understand the perceptions and fears of the Unionist community. The contacts and engagements themselves were helpful in promoting trust, and they undoubtedly influenced Sinn Fein as they developed their strategies.

The business and labor communities played a late, but effective role in the peace process. In the mid-1990s businesses began to co-operate with each other and with the trade unions to search for a more strategic approach that might pressure both republican and loyalist paramilitaries to end their campaigns of violence. Business and labor unions also publicly encouraged all parties to commit to political negotiations and participate in them. Groups including the Chamber of Commerce, the Confederation of British Industry, the Institute of Directors, and the trade unions participated in dialogues with Sinn Fein and with the Loyalist parties, often on economic issues. Their influence was helpful in addressing particular issues, and it played a valuable role in encouraging the political parties to enter into serious dialogue.

Many people from the United States during the 1990s also assisted in designing and sponsoring dialogue programs. Initially the U.S. dialogues were with Sinn Fein, but later dialogues also developed with the loyalist parties. In the 1990s many people from the U.S. began to experiment with a more inclusive process of dialogue, including all major parties to the conflict. Various Congressional and business representatives brought pressure to bear upon Sinn Fein to end violence, enter into dialogue, and engage with the Unionist community. President Bill Clinton and Senator George Mitchell played particularly important roles in promoting such dialogue efforts, and Mitchell became chairman for the multiparty talks that eventually produced an inclusive agreement between the parties.

In reflecting on the many informal, off-the-record initiatives that led up to and supported the formal negotiations, it is clear that they played a powerful role in the peace process. Part of the reason they had this impact was the broad base of individuals and groups that participated in them, and part was a result of their persistence and intensity of interaction. But perhaps most important, especially toward the end, was their understanding that for the entire enterprise to succeed, no major stakeholder could be excluded, even the paramilitary groups that did not renounce violence until the very end.

The latter point is especially important. Ending violence is an obvious, essential objective of formal peace negotiations, and the wider the renunciation of violence, the stronger the chances that a peace agreement will endure. The experience in Northern Ireland reveals how it is possible to get all major players to re-nounce violence—by frequent informal contacts and engage-ment with groups *outside* the formal negotiations, building trust until they renounce violence, at which point they can be brought into the formal process. It is hard to end violence without get-ting groups committed to violence to stop it. And it is hard to get them to stop without some way of communicating with them and ultimately including them in formal negotiations. In Northern Ireland, these groups were the paramilitary groups; in the Middle East it is many groups, including Hamas, Islamic Jihad, Hesbollah, Al Qaeda, and others.

Recruiting Citizens for Peace in South Africa

On February 2, 1990, nine days before Nelson Mandela was released from prison, South African President F.W. de Klerk opened Parliament with a speech that announced the end of apartheid and a new beginning for his country. "It is time for us to break out of the cycle of violence and to break through to peace and reconciliation," he said; and he committed

his government and the country to "a new democratic constitution, universal franchise . . . and equality before an independent judiciary."[8] In the speech he ended the bans on several organizations, including the African National Congress (ANC); he
affirmed his commitment to the release of political prisoners and
the end of restrictions on more than thirty organizations; and
he announced the release of Mandela.

In the months that followed, violence borne of centuries of
oppression escalated throughout the country. Apartheid was being dismantled, but there was nothing to take its place, and the
country was spiraling out of control.

In the winter of 1991 the South African Council of Churches
(SACC) tried to take the lead in controlling violence, but conflict between Zulu leader Mangosuthu Buthelezi and the ANC
aborted the initiative. Business leaders, working through the
Consultative Business Movement (CBM), tried their hands. In
April, President de Klerk called a summit for late May, but the
ANC refused to participate. In the end it was church and business leaders who worked out a plan that brought both the government and the ANC to the table at the summit.

Assisted in important ways by the South African trade unions, this was the background for drafting the National Peace
Accord, which was made public at a National Peace Convention
on September 14, 1991. The Accord was a pact among twenty-
six of the country's leading institutions to stop the violence. It
established a space for a culture of informal conflict resolution
to transform the country's culture of violence. It provided for
creation of peace committees operating at every level of government—national, regional, and local. These committees provided
mechanisms for people from all sectors to work together with

8. Susan Collin Marks, *Watching the Wind* (Washington, D.C.: United
States Institute of Peace Press, 2000), 4–5.

adversaries on building a new society. The process there was entirely a citizens' movement, in which the government was simply one among many players. One may assume the reason the government played no special role is that only citizens' organizations coming together could command the respect and trust necessary for the process to work.

Susan Collin Marks, in her book *Watching the Wind*, describes the importance of this initiative, preparing the country for its first election in April 1994:

> [A]s the peace process got under way, something extraordinary happened. The forces of democratization adopted and adapted the conflict resolution tools, the problem-solving techniques, and the facilitating skills that form the essence of the peacemaking process. Conflict resolution spread as an agent of change on a mass scale at multiple levels.[9]

Ms. Marks tells how, after the fall of apartheid, citizens came to share responsibility for maintaining the peace. She tells her story in the most intimate way, relating how people off all races and religions mobilized to anticipate violence and to contain it once started. In one particularly memorable moment, at an angry meeting of 700 that went on for seven hours, an extraordinary exchange occurred between a police officer and a peace committee fieldworker.[10] During the introductions, the police officer introduced himself, and the fieldworker then replied: "I know you. You tortured me in Worcester in 1986." Ms. Marks describes what happened next:

> They looked at each other across the room and the years, remembering. The fieldworker had risked his life fighting against apartheid. . . . [T]he policeman had . . . crossed that porous line into the murky underworld of torture, knowing

9. Ibid., p. 10.
10. Ibid., p. 27.

that, despite the illegality of torture, his actions would be tac-
itly condoned by the state and his superiors. . . . Now the
peace structures had brought together these former enemies.
. . . The inconceivable was happening in this very room, and
in rooms like this all over the country, as more and more
people came together across the deep divides that character-
ized our land and made it a pariah in the world community.

This citizen initiative was a major reason why South Africa
maintained relative peace at a time when most people expected
a bloodbath. It succeeded as it persuaded people that if South
Africa was to have any future, it would have to be built on an
understanding that all could win, that there didn't need to be
losers in the new society. This was a tall order indeed in light
of the recent history there, but it succeeded overall.

The intensive, informal dialogue that occurred in South Africa from 1991 until 1994, when the country's first elections took
place, played an important role in its movement toward democracy. Without formal negotiations there could be no peace, no
transfer of power, no real democracy. But without the informal,
citizen-based initiatives focused on maintaining the peace
throughout the country, there is little doubt the entire experience would have imploded into chaos and violence.

These informal dialogues, undertaken within the National
Peace Accord, helped pave the way for elections. The Peace and
Reconciliation Commission, which was launched in 1996 continued these informal activities building trust and forgiveness so
that democracy could succeed.[11]

11. The Peace and Reconciliation Commission was the subject of an extraordinary film, In My Country—starring Samuel L. Jackson and Juliet Bino-
che—and produced in 2005 by Robert L. Chartoff, Mike Medavoy, John Boorman, Kieran Corrigan, and Lynn Hendee; and directed by John Boorman.

Reducing Conflict
in Burundi

Decades of ethnic conflict and violence veered out
of control and erupted into genocide in Rwanda in 1994, when
the majority Hutus slaughtered more than half a million Tutsis
and moderate Hutus.[12] The international community feared a
repeat of the genocide in Burundi next door. Washington-based
Search for Common Ground (Search) became involved in trying
to reduce ethnic conflict in Burundi a year later; and for nearly
a decade since then, it has played a key role in reducing conflict
there.

Search launched its Burundi operations in 1995 with the
country's first independent radio production outlet, Studio
Ijambo, in the capital Bujumbura. Search has found radio to be
effective in fostering dialogue and peace-building in a region
where radio is often people's only access to reliable information.
It established Studio Ijambo to provide balanced and anti-in-
flammatory broadcasting countering "hate radio" and pervasive
rumors. Using an interethnic team of journalists, the studio produces a variety of programs that facilitate dialogue and reconciliation among Burundians. The programs include educational
media programming, professional training for journalists, and
promotion of inclusive participation, especially for women and
youths, in the nation's peace process.

Search also promotes dialogue, reconciliation, and peace in
other formats, including soap opera, news magazines, call-in
shows, documentaries, and short clips. Because its programs are
seen as neither Hutu nor Tutsi dominated, more than nine out
of ten Burundians turn to Studio Ijambo for reliable and objective information.

12. The actual number is disputed, with a range between 500–800,000.

But the studio does more than provide information. One high-ranking government official explained its impact: "Another important role is their interviews and talks with the various fighting factions during their fight. When people fight, they do not stop to understand each other's needs. . . . S[tudio] I[jambo] helps them hear each other's needs and issues; this facilitates negotiations, and puts an end to the fight."[13]

In 1999, Search started working with youth by engaging young Hutu and Tutsi ex-combatants. Working closely with the local organization JAMAA, Search helped a core group of three young people to reconcile with one another. This work led to initiation of a series of informal gatherings and even soccer tournaments, which brought many more young people together for the first time. As they got to know each other, they started looking for ways to raise the awareness of the new younger generation in Burundi so they wouldn't repeat past mistakes. This was a sensitive task because of taboos on discussing the role that elites had played in manipulating youth to participate in ethnic violence.

The multi-ethnic youth group came up with the idea of using books to tell true stories, but under fictional names, about how they were lured into extremist movements at a young age, the heavy prices they paid for the choices they made, and the efforts they were making to re-build their lives and their societies together. The Burundian Education Ministry adopted the books for use in the national school system. Hutu and Tutsi pairs of the youth group then read the books with classes of students and discussed their experiences to warn the students from making the same mistakes. The youth group won a special award from UNESCO for peace-building.

13. Amr Abdalla, et al., *Independent Program Evaluation: Search for Common Ground in Burundi* (An Evaluation Report to Search for Common Ground, Washington, DC, February, 1999).

More recently, Search's youth program helped build capacity for conflict resolution in a secondary school in the district of Kayanza. Serious violence based on ethnic divisions arose when students were to elect their class representatives. A Search intervention facilitated creation of a conflict resolution club at the school and then trained students effectively to manage their club. Because of the club's involvement, two student leaders who were previously enemies (a Tutsi and a Hutu) have come to be seen as exemplary of positive collaboration within the school compound.

Studio Ijambo's radio shows have continued to play an important role in reducing conflict. One activity that has been especially noteworthy is "Heroes' Summit." This grew out of a weekly radio series which told the stories of "heroes"—Hutus who had saved the lives of Tutsis, and Tutsis who had saved Hutus. The aim was to redefine what it means to be a "hero." In April 2004, Studio Ijambo sponsored a "Heroes Summit." This event publicly highlighted and honored the stories of nearly two hundred Burundians who, in moments of extreme crisis and ethnic violence, risked their lives to save people of different ethnic groups. Individual "heroes" took the stage and thanked those who saved their lives in stories sometimes dating as far back as 1972. Since the Summit the word *Inkingi*, which roughly translates in English as "public-spiritedness"—describing people committing acts of humanity and solidarity—has become part of everyday Burundian vocabulary.

A school teacher expressed the feelings of many people in the following statement, sent to Studio Ijambo:

> The world is full of people famous for their bad deeds. But there are others who act with their heart and faith, but we hardly know them. Studio Ijambo has taken these numerous heroes from the shadows and presented them in front of the

nation as the genuine flames of peace and reconciliation for Burundi.

Search also sponsors the Women's Peace Centre (WPC) and the Youth Project (YP) to facilitate community reconciliation through meetings, exchanges, and joint projects in which people from different groups meet and work with their neighbors, often for the first time in years. The WPC's first director, Sandra Melone, who initiated this hands-on approach, was determined to do more than organize seminars about conflict transformation and inter-ethnic cooperation. Through this and other projects, the WPC has popularized the term "positive (or inter-ethnic) solidarity" while providing forums for expressing constructive proposals in community gatherings.

In 2004 these gatherings culminated in a "Pardon and Reconciliation Day" in Ngozi Province. Speaking at the event, the governor of the province, Mr. Juvénal Nzigamasabo, who was suspicious at first about the meeting, abandoned his prepared speech and spoke spontaneously to the crowd: "What you are doing is the real life application of the peace accords." He concluded: "The leaders have signed cease-fire agreements, but you have done a cease fire in your hearts. The Truth and Reconciliation Commission will use this community as an example."

Notwithstanding the serious challenges Burundi still faces, there is no question that great progress has been made over the past decade. In 1995 there were no independent radio outlets, no peace negotiations, hardly any involvement of women in trying to make peace, and even speaking about ethnic tension was taboo. Today, five independent radio stations are operating, together with a vibrant women's movement, open discussions of Hutu and Tutsi identity, full negotiations that led to a flawed but nevertheless productive peace process, and a transitional government. All of these projects have contributed to bringing about a paradigm shift in Burundian society. For the first time in decades, people dare to believe in a life without war.

Working with local partners, Search was a key contributor to this progress through its work in Burundi. It also continues to support the Burundian peace process by keeping the Great Lakes region of Africa on the agenda of policymakers and the NGO community in Washington. For almost a decade Search, working with partner organizations, has organized a monthly policy forum in Washington, D.C. It has, more recently, been convening a similar forum for Europeans in Brussels (Le Forum European pour les Grands Lacs). The forums provide an opportunity for representatives of government and non-government agencies, diplomatic corps, and international organizations to focus on the Great Lakes region, share experiences and opinions, and receive the latest information and views from people on the ground.

David Callahan, writing in *CivNet Journal*, expressed the view of many observers in 1998: "Events in Burundi over the past four years provide a clear-cut example of where NGOs have played a decisive role in heading off a major war."

Civic Engagement as a New Front in the War on Terrorism

Peace, to be sustainable, needs to reach beyond the letter of agreements to their spirit. The letter of agreements is always about a negative concept of peace—reducing or ending conflict. The spirit of agreements is about a positive concept of what it is to be peaceful. Official negotiations can address both letter and spirit—especially by insisting that both are important—but they need informal engagement really to strengthen the spirit—to create a culture of peace.

The examples of India, Northern Ireland, South Africa, and Burundi demonstrate the power of personal engagement and society-based initiatives in promoting the positive spirit of peace, supporting official peace initiatives. These are but four of many in which citizen engagement played a significant role in reducing conflicts that were of great, official concern.

Despite evidence of the power of personal contact and engagement in reducing conflict from all regions of the world, recent peace initiatives in the Middle East have paid no more than lip service to informal engagement in official initiatives for peace there. The sequence of analyses about why nothing seems to work for peace in the Middle East tells an interesting story of a shifting target in an analysis focused only on states, which has not changed very much despite continuing disappointment at the results of peace initiatives there. Unfortunately, the failure to see beyond states to societies may end up in tragedy.

The state-focused analysis of both Israel and the United States first blamed Arafat for the failure to achieve peace. With Arafat's passing, the analysis shifted to *democracy* as the key to peace.[14] Now that the Palestinians have elected their first president and have democracy, that is seen to be falling short; and the Israelis are saying, in effect, democracy is not enough: the new democracy needs to do more in fighting the terrorists. The Israelis are pushing the new, fragile democracy to solve the challenge of societies and end terrorism, and the Americans often implicitly assent by saying nothing. At best, President Abbas may achieve a fragile success. At worst—if he is pushed to do things

14. In terms of our argument, democracy *would* be the key to peace if it included commitment to citizen empowerment and society-based initiatives to help support formal peace negotiations. Unfortunately, many of those who emphasize democracy tend to limit their definition of democracy to voting, without emphasizing the role of citizens in sharing responsibility for making peace and sustaining it.

he has no power to do—his government and the new Palestinian democracy will collapse, and the Palestinian leadership will go by default to radical extremist factions. Secretary of State Condoleeza Rice expressed this same concern last summer.[15]

This could happen if we overload this government's capacity to perform by asking things that are impossible for it. The real failing here is the failure to understand the limits of state action, the need to understand societies as problems independent from states, and the need to commit to society-based initiatives to address problems rooted in societies.

Some of the fragile states that have become national security problems are fragmented by tribal, ethnic, or religious loyalties. These are states in which societies are substantially independent of states. Many of them are security problems for the international community. Connection and engagement of citizens along lines discussed here in relation to peace can provide a powerful antidote to the tribal or ethnic loyalties, encouraging consciousness beyond one's own group to others. This is a large and important, additional effect of activities engaging and connecting people for peace.

What is needed is a consistent, sustained effort to recruit citizens as partners in the peace process. In Northern Ireland over more than a decade, in South Africa, and wherever peace has been found between Hindus and Muslims in India for almost fifty years, one of the dominant realities to be understood is the limitations and weakness of states. These and other examples also show that strategies aiming at negative peace—peace understood as the absence of conflict—are unstable at best; they show that true peace had to emerge from *society* in the form of a *positive peace* forged from engagement and trust.

---

15. Aluf Benn, "Rice Concerned a Weakened Abbas Could Lose Grip on Gaza," *Haaretz*, July 24, 2005.

Society-based initiatives, aimed at engaging citizens, will ordinarily be directed at leadership groups: opinion leaders in business, labor, religious institutions, media leaders, and others. Religious leaders are especially important in many places, including the Middle East. An especially interesting program for religious leaders was organized by peace activist Stephen P. Cohen in early 2005. The conference was structured as a dialogue between religious teachers and leaders representing the Muslim, Jewish, Catholic, Evangelical Protestant, and Greek Orthodox religions. The objective was to begin the task of building "a cohort of religious leaders who will preach and teach their own faithful in words and acts that come to build respect and unlearn contempt." The meeting was, by all accounts, a great success, and it should be repeated, with meetings both in the U.S. and in the Middle East, with religious leaders talking about a wide variety of subjects in addition to peace.

The real issue is the need for a strong commitment to community-based initiatives to supplement and support formal peace negotiations. For such initiatives to make a real impact in promoting peace, whether in the Middle East or anywhere else, three conditions are necessary: first, they must be mounted at scales sufficient to have an impact; second, they must be formally endorsed and embraced as part of the official peace process by the principal, official parties to the conflict; and finally, they must aim, through civil society initiatives, to go beyond the absence of conflict to a positive culture of peace. Unless these conditions are satisfied, community-based initiatives promoting peace will have only limited impact in changing societies. The dedication of governments to commit to these initiatives and to encourage their citizens to do so is in fact a good litmus test of their real commitment to peace—of their willingness to move beyond words to action.

The key to all changes examined here—whether economic

policy reform or girls' education or peace—is local ownership of the need for change. In the case of peace, the cause must be "owned" not only by the governments involved in the dispute but also by citizens on both sides. Formal sanctioning of society-based initiatives is important because without a formal endorsement people will be implicitly encouraged (by the omission) to believe that informal, Track Two efforts are not important. In such a case, people will get the message that only the *letter* of a peace agreement matters, not the spirit. The objective, however, is not only to achieve peace; it is also to be *peaceful*, and that requires following both the letter and the spirit.

*   *   *

Although this chapter has focused on the challenges of peace and reducing conflict, we want to note that in many respects the challenge of promoting democracy is similar to—and even depends on—reducing conflict and promoting trust. Discussions of democracy frequently focus on formal institutions such as voting, but informal factors such as trust and some measure of political consensus are also important for the operation of functioning democracies. For this reason, the engagement strategies discussed above for peace also have powerful, potential uses in promoting the trust, connection, and consensus that are crucial preconditions to developing democracy in many countries.

5. Roles of Civil Society during and after Conflicts

Since the end of the Cold War, a "hot peace" of escalating community conflicts, guerrilla violence, and regional wars has occurred, resulting in great loss of life and the destruction of institutions of government, civil society, and the private sector in all regions of the world. The international news media focus mainly on major wars and their aftermath, such as the continuing violence in Afghanistan and Iraq, but tend to overlook the fact that more than one-third of the nations in the world are affected by conflicts. By mid-2004, more than seventy-five nations were experiencing armed conflicts or were in post-crisis transition. If one adds other countries housing large refugee populations, and those suffering from recurrent natural disasters and the HIV/AIDS pandemic, at least 110 countries—well over 50 percent of the nations of the world—are ravaged by increasing instability, resource challenges, disease, and ultimately, chaos.

Yet more nations are expected to experience conflict in the near future. Most of them also have high levels of severe poverty, with families living on less than one dollar a day. They usually have large "youth bulges," with unskilled, illiterate, and unemployed youth fomenting instability.

These countries have become the seedbed of revolutionaries seeking to redress extreme socio-economic, educational, and

ethnic inequities, of international terrorists leading violent economic and religious revitalization movements, and of criminal
groups managing illicit international trades (e.g., trade in drugs,
arms, human workers, abusive child labor, sexual slaves, and natural resources such as diamonds, minerals, protected animals,
etc.). Because remote lawless regions in many countries of South
and Southeast Asia, the former Soviet Union, Latin America,
and Sub-Saharan Africa are exceedingly difficult to control, they
also serve as refuges, training camps, and even killing fields for
guerrillas, paramilitaries, and many violent international groups.

These new realities create an urgent priority to develop new
approaches to mitigating conflict and the effects of conflict in
these societies.

Most specialists writing about nations with conflicts focus
on their fragile governments, discussing them in terms of "state
failure." This perspective is part of the habit, which we have
discussed on other issues, of seeing only states and not seeing
societies separately from states. As in other arenas that we have
discussed, society-based initiatives, implemented by national and
local civil society organizations (CSOs), can play an important
role in reducing conflict and mitigating the effects of conflict.
For this reason, we should review the experiences of nations that
have used civil society approaches successfully to overcome internal conflict.

Because they are "the citizens' institutions," national and local CSOs are often the most important—and unheralded—actors for mitigating conflict as well as the effects of conflict and
ensuring protection and education of the young.[1] In times of
violence and stress, national CSOs help maintain critical, fragile

1. E. Vargas-Barón and M. McClure, "The New Heroics of Generational
Commitment: Education in Nations with Chronic Crises," in *Education as a
Humanitarian Response* (London: Cassel and International Bureau of Education,
1998).

infrastructures that preserve essential elements of society, and they provide spaces for planning post-conflict reconstruction and development. After violence has ended, if adequately supported these institutions can play important roles in reforming broken institutions and achieving a durable peace. These roles are especially important in nations designated as "fragile" or "failed" states. Strengthening CSOs will attack the roots of violence, empowering people directly affected by conflict to develop strategies appropriate to local cultures for pacifying violent regions.

Key CSOs during and after conflicts include:

- Administrative and managerial associations for business development and economic productivity;

- Educational institutions, including parenting programs, preschool education, vocational education for ex-combatants and unemployed youth;

- Programs for health, nutrition, and persons with disabilities;

- Organizations promoting legal rights and essential services for vulnerable children, refugees, and internally displaced persons;

- Agricultural and rural development and urban rehabilitation programs and institutes; and

- Programs for environmental protection, water and waste disposal, and many others.

During crises, national CSOs provide continuing employment for professionals and other program personnel, thus helping them remain in their country. The "brain drain" that has occurred in virtually all conflict nations results in an enormous loss of national specialists, whose expertise is essential for internal reform and reconstruction. When they leave, their institutions are further weakened, leading to a loss of the "critical mass" that is crucial for rebuilding society and the economy. Nations that lose this critical mass of technicians, as Colombia did in the late 1940s and 1950s, experience a weakening of their institutions and then never fully recover during the post-conflict period, often leading to cyclical violence.

CSOs help establish or maintain communications between communities and government at all levels, especially when those governments are fragile or transitory. Perhaps most importantly, these institutions can promote and lead planning activities during conflict, and then participate in planning major governmental reforms during the critical eighteen to twenty-four month "window of opportunity" in the period immediately after the conflict ends. After that, if no reform occurs, nations tend to revert to "comfortable" if dysfunctional systems. National CSOs should play important roles at all levels in consultations and consensus building, which are important for promoting policy reforms, preparing annual action plans, and passing enforcement legislation. They should help forge partnerships between government and non-state institutions in all sectors and geographical areas, including international CSOs and bilateral and multilateral donors.

The nature, size, strength, and roles of institutions of civil society vary greatly from region to region. In North, Central, and South America, Europe, Australia, New Zealand, and parts of Africa, national CSOs are very strong. In other regions with long traditions of highly centralized government control, authoritarian rule or state socialism, CSOs have been developed more recently and tend to be fewer in number and less-experienced. In nations of the former Soviet Union, East and South Asia, and much of the Middle East, CSOs have increased in number recently due mainly to governmental, religious or international sponsorship. Institutional, political, and cultural conditions determine how national CSOs can be used for helping reduce conflict and achieve durable peace.

The Roles of Civil Society Organizations during and after Conflicts: Alternative Models

A variety of models and roles exist for CSOs during and after conflicts. While many people believe it is impossible to develop programs during conflicts, some programs have been very effective in giving services to displaced persons, especially in education and training. More common are programs launched in the crucial eighteen- to twenty-four-month period after a conflict ends. Among the more important of these are programs aimed at retraining ex-combatants and providing education to children deprived of education during the conflict. Some of these initiatives grew out of partnerships between CSOs and governments; others were initiated by CSOs without any government participation at all. Programs focusing on education and training ranged from basic education to training for employment to conflict resolution to education for democracy and human rights. Following are thumbnail sketches of a few civil society models.[2]

El Salvador

El Salvador is still recovering from the ravages of a twelve-year civil war in the 1980s that ended with the signing of peace accords in 1992. The country suffered profound infrastructural

---

2. These case studies are presented in: Vargas-Barón, E. and H. Bernal Alacón, eds., *From Bullets to Blackboards: Education for Peace in Latin America and Asia* (Washington, D.C.: Inter-American Development Bank, 2005).

damage as national development was subordinated to a war agenda that severely weakened governmental and civil society institutions. When the civil war in El Salvador ended in January 1992, over 30,000 guerrillas and government soldiers, including both men and women, were dismissed to rejoin society. They had known nothing but hatred and violence for years. Many were illiterate or functionally illiterate, and they lacked the skills and material resources required to develop enterprises.[3] The following discussion focuses on two efforts to overcome some of the effects of the conflict: The Program for the Reintegration and Employment of Ex-Combatants, designed by a national CSO, the Salvadoran Pro-Rural Health Association (ASAPRO-SAR) with the support of German development agency GTZ; and a comprehensive educational reform program that began before the conflict ended.

The ASAPROSAR program created and expanded job and income-earning opportunities for ex-combatants, and helped them establish individual and group micro-enterprises. Through facilitating instructional processes in dressmaking, tailoring, and rural health services, 225 ex-combatants, 80 percent of whom were women, were able to rejoin society. The program featured a unique model with an educational philosophy and new methodologies that emphasized comprehensive human development, training for citizenship, and building positive inter-personal relations while providing work skills and job opportunities. The program was accredited in 1996 as a Collaborating Center of the Salvadoran Professional Training Institute (INSAFORP) and it became a model for other programs and for the nation's Institutional Policy on Education-Training that was developed

---

3. E. Guzman de Luna, "Reintegrating Ex-Combatants into Society in El Salvador" in *From Bullets to Blackboards: Education for Peace in Latin America and Asia*, eds. E. Vargas-Barón and H. Bernal Alarcón (Washington, D.C.: Inter-American Development Bank, 2005).

in 1999. Typical of many national CSO leadership efforts, ASA-PROSAR proved to be a sustainable institution. It continues to serve conflict-affected communities and develop innovative programs that meet evolving socio-economic needs in rural El Salvador. Though small, this model for reintegrating ex-combatants into society had a major impact in El Salvador.

During the war, investment in education declined, many schools were destroyed, teachers were in scarce supply, and the complex bureaucracy of the Ministry of Education became even slower in its programming, and more centralized and more highly politicized than ever. Most rural poor and other marginalized populations received no education at all during the war.

While the conflict was still raging in 1989, planning began for a comprehensive national education reform, and by 1992 the reform process was ready to become part of a general post-conflict reconstruction effort. Its purpose was to achieve more equitable economic development, strengthen democracy, and promote sustainable peace.[4] Leadership for this participatory process of educational reform resided not only in the Ministry of Education, but also the national university and other institutions of civil society and community-based organizations that worked in partnership with the government to plan and rebuild the education system. Harvard University, USAID, and other bilateral and multilateral donors provided technical support. Salvadoran leaders of civil society (as well as government) worked together to set priorities and establish new strategies, program areas, indicators, and targets. El Salvador's educational reform program included pre-school, primary, and secondary education for the poorest populations; enlarged and improved the network

4. J. L. Guzman, "Educational Reform in Post-War El Salvador" in *From Bullets to Blackboards: Education for Peace in Latin America and Asia*, eds. E. Vargas-Barón and H. Bernal Alarcón (Washington, D.C.: Inter-American Development Bank, 2005).

of schools; developed non-formal literacy, basic education, and skills training for youth and adults; improved curriculum quality and teacher training; provided revised educational materials for teachers and students; improved the quality of tertiary education; decentralized administrative services; provided scholarships; and encouraged private sector participation.

Although some international level specialists assert it is impossible to consult communities during and immediately after conflicts, this reform included such consultations and proved to be one of the world's most participatory and successful educational policy planning processes. The Salvadoran conflict was exceedingly violent. The Salvadoran education reform movement demonstrates that even under the most difficult of circumstances, large-scale consultation and consensus building can be conducted successfully soon after a conflict ends.[5]

5. In contrast to the educational planning experience in El Salvador, case studies of education reforms in Lao People's Democratic Republic (PDR) and Vietnam demonstrate that unless policy planning is conducted soon after the cessation of conflict, major educational inequities will remain for many years leading to grave national problems that can—and have—lead to a renewal of conflict. In Lao PDR, it took many years for the government to realize that a decentralized in-service teacher training system was needed to provide better educational quality for remote, often culturally distinct rural villages. Rural violence has been increasing due largely to inequities affecting minority ethnic groups living in these remote regions. Although a nation-wide teacher training process has been led by a centralized ministerial structure, the system is highly decentralized. Community development organizations are contributing significantly to program success and provide in-kind assistance for local teachers.

Similarly, after the war, Viet Nam's centralized government focused on providing educational services for cities and easy to access rural population zones. They generally disregarded remote rural villages and thousands of war orphans became unschooled street children. These inequities led to a large unmet demand for educational services in remote areas. Street children came to be regarded as juvenile delinquents and many were killed as a public menace. In the 1990s, in its effort to achieve universal primary education, Viet Nam instituted a program of Multigrade Education in remote areas and developed the Alternative Basic Education (ABE) program for street children. The former depends largely upon civil society support for the schools, and the ABE pro-

Colombia

During the recent period of violence in the region of Tolima in Colombia, the epicenter of early guerrilla movements, the University of Ibagué has developed a semi-independent community college that provides internally displaced populations with quality basic education, citizenship education, an array of technical skills training courses, and classes on small and medium business development.[6] It has partnered with national and regional private enterprises to meet emerging needs for trained workers, thereby ensuring jobs for unemployed youth and adults.

The University of Ibagué has forged partnerships with the government to develop virtual learning centers in remote towns located in violence zones. The centers provide in-service teacher training, classes for primary and secondary school students, skills training to meet local needs, and citizenship training. This service has helped stem the tide of internal displacement and has given hope to families facing violence on a daily basis. The uni-

---

gram has achieved strong support from communities, local associations, and temples that provide accessible learning spaces for street children.

As demonstrated in El Salvador, it is critically important to begin planning for an education reform during or immediately after a conflict, with the strong participation of civil society. Because they waited for many years to reform their education systems and lacked strong civil society institutions, Lao PDR and Viet Nam have had to deal with sporadic violence and low levels of formal education that have limited national productivity, denied full citizenship to vulnerable children in impoverished minority communities, and neglected the educational and support needs of vulnerable children. See S. Lachanthaboun, K. Phomsavanh, and A. Thomas, "Teacher Training in Remote Areas of Lao PDR" and D. V. Than, "Educating Hard-to-Reach Children in Viet Nam" in E. Vargas-Barón and H. Bernal Alarcón, editors (2005). *From Bullets to Blackboards: Education for Peace in Latin America and Asia.* Washington, DC: Inter-American Development Bank.

    6. H. Bernal Alarcón, L. F. Bernal Villegas and L. López Herrán, "Building a Laboratory for Peace" in *From Bullets to Blackboards: Education for Peace in Latin America and Asia*, eds. E. Vargas-Barón and H. Bernal Alarcón (Washington, D.C.: Inter-American Development Bank, 2005).

versity also trains teachers in methods of trauma healing, conflict resolution, and mediation. Most recently, it is developing a productivity center for training rural workers in new agricultural techniques for use when they will be able to return home. They are also designing quality primary schools with enriched contents and new educational methods to meet special psychosocial needs of children and families affected by violence.

The University of Ibagué has maintained separate cost centers for each program, ensured transparent and fully accountable financial and program processes, evaluated and monitored its programs, and achieved stated results. By investing in this innovative regional university and its courageous and creative personnel, the Government of Colombia, international sponsors principally from the U.S. and Europe, and local industries are helping strengthen this civil society institution, maintain essential education services during a stressful and dangerous period, and build a competent base for post-violence reconstruction and development. This evidence-based program model could be adapted and replicated in many parts of the world.

Philippines

Many have posited that quality education cannot be achieved during a conflict. However, with support from Oxfam, a national CSO in the Philippines, the Community of Learners Foundation (COLF), is successfully helping a large public school system in violence-plagued Mindanao to expand and improve its services for internally displaced populations and residents.[7] The education program includes: in-service training for teachers, other

7. F. de los Angeles-Bautista, "Creating Schools that Heal and Teach Peace in the Philippines" in *From Bullets to Blackboards: Education for Peace in Latin America and Asia*, eds. E. Vargas-Barón and H. Bernal Alarcón (Washington, D.C.: Inter-American Development Bank, 2005).

school personnel, parents and community volunteers; the provision of priority resources; program coordination, planning, needs assessments; monitoring and evaluating activities; and building community involvement in the schools, including organizing a Parent-Teacher-Community Association, and construction of school infrastructure.

Similar to the University of Ibagué, the COLF program demonstrates that even in the midst of war, teachers, other educational personnel, and the community can begin to transform public schools into effective, safe, and responsive learning environments. During the 2002–2003 school year, the program supported eleven elementary schools serving a total of 8,053 schoolchildren affected by the ongoing conflict. Evaluations have shown that there has been a notable increase in children's interest in learning and attendance. School personnel, including principals and supervisors, have become an effective team committed to and competent in facilitating student-oriented learning. The community became involved and contributed to the program's successes and has gained skills for influencing policies in the future to meet people's needs. The program provides a good example of how partnerships that are established between government and institutions of civil society can benefit children, families, and schools in crisis situations.

Guatemala

Similarly, Guatemala's ethnic Mayan populations were disproportionately affected by national conflicts from 1954 to December 26, 1996, the date when peace agreements were signed. As a result of their ethnic minority status, most Mayan Indians live in severe poverty in rural areas. Over 70 percent of rural women are illiterate, especially Mayan women. Mayan men tend to be more literate because of migrant labor or war experiences that included learning to read and write. Planning for a major effort to increase literacy began in 1997, well within the critical window of opportunity for overcoming the effects of conflicts. Under the umbrella of the Government's National Committee for Literacy Teaching, the Mayan Community Literacy (COMAL) Project was highly successful in expanding literacy and reducing the school dropout rate.[8] COMAL was funded by the U.S. Agency for International Development (USAID) through a contract with Save the Children/USA that provided technical support and served about 35,560 young Mayan women.[9] They participated in 2,553 study groups in more than 1,100 communities in fifty counties. COMAL provided services in communities through building a network of Guatemalan CSOs that received training on how to use a curriculum that combines literacy teaching and community development. The methodology is based on the participant's experiences and features active literacy-teaching processes.

COMAL offers an effective model for achieving cultural, linguistic, and ethnic relevance. Although the COMAL Project has been closed because external funding support ended, program contents and methods continue to be used by many Guatemala CSOs and other institutions. Once again, national institutions of civil society can help ensure sustainable services. COMAL demonstrates that integrated bilingual education programs for marginalized ethnic minorities can be developed successfully in the wake of a prolonged civil war.

8. H. Estrada Armas, "Promoting Literacy and Women's Development in Mayan Communities in Guatemala" in *From Bullets to Blackboards: Education for Peace in Latin America and Asia*, eds. E. Vargas-Barón and H. Bernal Alarcón (Washington, D.C.: Inter-American Development Bank, 2005).

9. COMAL used the standardized Integrated Community Literacy Teaching methodology.

Indonesia

International support can and sometimes should be provided directly to viable education programs developed during and after conflicts by national civil society organizations that have not formed a partnership with government. Since 1999, Ambon, the capital city of the Maluku Islands, located in the eastern part of Indonesia, has suffered from ongoing sectarian conflict between Muslims and Christians. At the height of these communal conflicts, about 300,000 persons were displaced from the city and surrounding areas, and many have continued to live in camps or other public facilities originally set up to meet short-term emergency needs. The conflicts destroyed many schools and playgrounds; consequently, children have suffered greatly, both physically and psychologically. Young children played in the only space they had: camp gutters. They often exhibited extreme symptoms of fear and aggression, and had poor concentration and low self-esteem. Drug use and street children emerged.

Initially in the Ambon area, early childhood education was considered unimportant for poor families. The LAPPAN Program (The Foundation of Women's and Children's Empowerment) is a local CSO established by Indonesian professionals and affected parents to deal with the plight of young Islamic children in camps and villages. It provides high-quality early childhood development activities for children under six years of age as well as parent education and support.[10] The program also helps create bridges to parents in the Christian community, introduces international concepts of child development and education, uses

10. B. Tualeka, S. I. Erisandy and L. Iskandar-Dharmawan, "Early Childhood Development for Refugee Children in Indonesia" in *From Bullets to Blackboards: Education for Peace in Latin America and Asia*, eds. E. Vargas-Barón and H. Bernal Alarcón (Washington, D.C.: Inter-American Development Bank, 2005).

local learning toys and stories, and seeks to build effective life skills, including respect for others, self-confidence, and self-reliance. It offers a positive alternative to traditional regional education practices of rote learning and corporal punishment. The program uses research-based concepts of early childhood psychosocial stimulation to develop good learning skills, build memory capacity, and achieve balanced socio-emotional development. The program involves parents and community members in program design, implementation, and evaluation. It creates opportunities for children to learn through play, prepares them for formal schooling, and focuses on developing positive attitudes, cognitive abilities, knowledge, skills, and the creativity necessary to adapt to their challenging environment.

Quantitative evaluation data are not available as yet but qualitative observational data show that significant progress is being made. During the past four years, parental recognition of children's need to participate in early childhood education has increased, and the community has enabled more children and their parents to participate in the program. Children are exhibiting more positive behaviors and fewer psychological problems than before joining the program. Adults from ethnically diverse populations are learning how to work together and raise more tolerant children, and this should help to prevent future conflicts. In addition, this program model has been transferred to other communities and camps for displaced families, both Muslim and Christian.

Peru

The Peruvian program for "Training Community Leaders as Promoters of Human Rights, Democracy and Citizen Participation" provides a compelling example of a nationwide movement developed entirely by institutions of civil society to serve citizens subsequent to the decline of guerrilla groups in 1992.[11] It was designed and implemented by the Peruvian Institute of Education for Human Rights and Peace (IPEDEHP) to create a culture of respect for human rights and democracy. The program leaders, supported by several international donors, sought to counter the prevailing culture of violence and disrespect. Its main goals were to educate and empower community leaders through training workshops, help them learn to value human rights and democracy, and assist them to promote and implement these values in communities throughout Peru.

Between 1996 and 2001, the program trained 2,269 men and women leaders throughout the country as human rights promoters. Subsequently, they shared their training with over 96,976 violence-affected individuals. Evaluations reveal that the program increased participants' knowledge about human rights, created many local level human rights defense organizations, empowered community leaders to become human rights promoters, and fostered the reconciliation of groups alienated by conflicts. To feel fully independent and free to conduct its work for community empowerment, the program rejected governmental support and instead forged alliances with other national CSOs and community-based organizations, and accepted international funding support, especially from USAID.

11. R. M. Mujica, "Training Human Rights Promoters in Peru" in *From Bullets to Blackboards: Education for Peace in Latin America and Asia*, eds. E. Vargas-Barón and H. Bernal Alarcón (Washington, D.C.: Inter-American Development Bank, 2005).

Implications and Recommendations for U.S. Foreign and Development Policies

These successful policy reforms and education programs suggest a series of major lessons for U.S. foreign and development policies:

- It is feasible and advisable to promote civil society partnerships during and after conflicts, focusing especially on successful national CSOs and universities that have a track record of transparency and accountability. While international CSOs can play a supportive role, emphasis should be placed on the long-term role of national CSOs.

- Support for national policy planning to reform education systems should begin during a conflict or immediately after it in order to ensure rapid response to emerging educational needs at all levels.

- Special emphasis should be placed on ethnic minorities and vulnerable young children and youth.

- Processes for planning educational, early childhood and other social policies, action plans, and linked legislation can and should be highly participatory. They should include institutions of civil society at all levels.

- During conflicts, new investment strategies should be rapidly developed to support innovative institutions that are helping maintain civil society structures that will be important for planning and post-conflict development.

After conflicts, it is most important to support CSOs during the brief eighteen to twenty-four month window of opportunity for reforming education and other systems that contribute to the causes of conflict.

Conclusion

To preserve and build civil society organizations during and after conflicts, it is important to provide technical assistance and grants for participatory planning processes to achieve economic, educational, health, and other social reforms that will feature a strong role for national civil society institutions as well as the government. Governments tend to be transitory in conflict and immediate post-conflict periods. CSOs may be the thread of constancy in the midst of chaos.

The previous case studies show it is possible to give grants or contracts directly to institutions of civil society to provide programs for children and families for a variety of important programs during and after conflicts. It is especially strategic to invest in maintaining and strengthening national universities, community colleges, institutes, and CSOs that can maintain the fabric of civil society during conflicts and subsequently help lead development processes as soon as hostilities end.

Because of the negative impacts of violent conflict, grants and contracts should be awarded to CSOs that can provide trauma healing, teach human rights, build democratic processes, and resolve conflicts. Similarly, CSOs should be supported to serve ex-combatants with trauma healing, inter-personal skills development, and training on citizenship as well as skills for productive employment or developing enterprises.

Finally, CSOs will need financial investment and operational support, in-country and regional short-term training, and assistance in creating partnerships with sister institutions in other global regions. Over time, these investments will yield a cadre of experienced and knowledgeable specialists who can assist other nations seeking to end their conflicts and revitalize their societies.

6. Strategies for Reform

Since the end of the Cold War and especially since 9/11, non-state actors have become increasingly important in international affairs. We have argued that foreign policymakers need to respond to this development by working much more closely with civil society organizations as effective instruments for promoting economic, political, and social change in countries that have become threats to national and international security. Our purpose is to promote investments in civil society organizations at levels approaching their strategic value.

Once the foreign policy community recognizes the value of these new instruments, solutions will emerge to meet two other requirements: the need for serious investments in research and development to improve the organizations and their practices, and the need to create incentives for encouraging the transfer of knowledge about what works away from where it was created.

At present, unfortunately, few incentives exist to manage and communicate knowledge effectively, and this explains in part why there is little interest in supporting research to increase the economic and social impacts and political acceptability of particular initiatives. Military force is considered to be strategically important, so the U.S. and other countries invest billions of dollars in researching and developing weapons. The non-military instruments we are writing about have become strategically important, and now we need to invest in researching and developing them with the same seriousness that is applied to weapons development.

We have focused on several priorities for a new strategic aid policy. In conclusion, we review some additional issues and implications. We begin with the central objective of promoting civil society. We then address the need to work in fragile states; the importance of communication strategies; institutional, fiscal, and political challenges; knowledge and intelligence in the post-9/11 world; the need for bipartisanship; and the problem of social trust. We conclude with a note on the role of citizens in working with governments to solve major economic, political, and social challenges in the world that is emerging.

Relying on civil society organizations will provide an active strategy for promoting democracy in many countries, and it will do it in a way that honors and respects local institutions. It will also open important new spaces for meaningful, strategic engagement by middle-sized, and even small, donor countries in the international arena. It will help to build stronger bonds of friendship between the United States of America and nations throughout the world. Ultimately, investment in institutions of civil society will be very visible to people in rural communities as well as urban centers, and it should help to heal some of the raw wounds created by recent international conflicts.

Working through CSOs will be effective to accomplish strategic objectives for promoting social development (peace, educating girls) and changing state policies (economic and educational policy reform, property rights for the poor). Most importantly, working through local CSOs is key to achieving local ownership of the need for change.

The Challenge
of Working in
Fragile States

We are personally familiar with many projects in which citizens and CSOs have developed intimate relations with principals in situations that the U.S., other governments, and even the United Nations avoid, believing them beyond external influence. Examples include officials of American CSOs actively advising Soviet leaders in policy choices leading to the collapse of the USSR at the end of the 1990s, successful, private businessmen and CSOs in Colombia who privately visit remote rural areas to negotiate peace with Colombian guerrillas and self-defense leagues, and other, similar "impossible" situations.

Actions such as these have been largely invisible to the foreign policy community in the past. But invisible does not mean ineffectual. CSOs have played—and will continue to play—powerful roles in influencing conflict resolution and international relations, as well as foreign policy objectives. Policymakers need to find ways to engage this world of civil society initiatives to increase cooperation and the advantages that derive from it.

No matter how difficult it may seem to be to work in a failed, fragile or hostile state, CSOs can almost always find ways to build on what has been started by citizen groups of the country. A range of U.S. institutions, including the National Endowment for Democracy (NED), the Asia Foundation, and the Carter Center, has supported this kind of work. Agencies and institutions of other nations and also international organizations (most notably the United Nations) have also supported work in failed, fragile and hostile states.

However, the most powerful agents in this kind of work are local CSOs, which can achieve the local ownership of ideas that is crucial to success. Foreign policymakers need to establish lines of communication with these CSOs to begin this work, even in the most difficult and hostile countries, such as North Korea and Iran. In those few nations where there is a dearth of CSOs or their quality is questionable, it will be important to create strategies for developing and strengthening them.

Perception and Reality: The Need for Communication Strategies

Society-based initiatives aimed at promoting economic and social development can improve people's lives. Initiatives concerned with ending poverty, promoting democracy, and achieving social justice can achieve objective results that help people see more hopeful futures. In important ways, however, the *subjective* components of hope and a sense of possibility may, in the short term, be even more important than tangible progress toward objective goals such as democracy and the rule of law. With hope, violent impulses often abate rapidly.

Subjective issues are matters of *perception*. Perceptions can be either true or false, but in either case they will define what people *think* is true. Some perceptions, even though false, become security problems because they are believed. Because perceptions are so important, we need to develop strategies for communicating to major audiences—to citizens as well as government officials—the effectiveness of CSO initiatives, how they are improving the lives of people, and what they promise for people everywhere in the future. We need to tell people why civil society is so important in achieving peaceful change: empowering women, recruiting citizens for democracy and peace, creating property rights for everyone, and other key results for overcoming poverty and achieving sustainable development.

When the U.S. Government wants to communicate, the

government organization chart points to U.S. Government agencies, especially the Under Secretary for Public Diplomacy and Public Affairs of the Department of State. For the new post-9/11 challenge, we need a more believable communications strategy, one implemented not only by official U.S. Government agencies, but also by local civil society organizations in other countries. Official government communications have no possibility of creating local ownership. Communications from local sources have more authenticity and are more believable endorsements that the values we support are *universal* values—values in which everyone shares ownership.

Some of the programs discussed here, such as the media program of Search for Common Ground in Burundi, are themselves communication programs. They are helping to change people's perceptions. But *all* initiatives considered strategic need to be communicated to priority audiences.

To add communications programs to society-based initiatives will require a special effort because few CSOs—the Instituto Libertad y Democracia and Search for Common Ground are notable exceptions—have any skill or experience in social communications and policy advocacy. CSOs tend to lack this capacity because funders have created very limited demand for it.

Perceptions are especially crucial in relation to important subjective issues. Among these, one of the most significant is making people feel honored and valued. This is especially important in relation to Muslims and the Arab world, where the impulse to terrorism is fueled largely by feelings of disempowerment and humiliation. While the conflict between Palestinians and Israelis plays a paramount role in this problem, U.S. policies are also seen to be a cause of Arab humiliation. People who accuse the U.S. of being imperialistic express the rage of peoples who feel oppressed. It is irrelevant whether the perception is true or fair: as long as they feel oppressed, this feeling fuels revolutionary impulses and creates a national and international security problem.

Programs that create a sense that Arabs and Muslims are honored and valued are greatly needed. The dialogues discussed in chapter four, networking civil society organizations, provide powerful examples of how to do this. But beyond the need for initiatives that honor people is the need to *communicate* this reality widely to people who cannot experience it themselves firsthand, which means especially to Arab and Muslim peoples.

Implementation: Institutional, Political, and Fiscal Challenges

One of the greatest challenges in implementing our proposals will be to exercise the patience and discipline to move forward in a systematic way, guided by serious research and development. We will have failed if our argument only leads to a frenzy of spending on non-strategic aid programs. In that event, disappointment will quickly follow—a sense of lost possibilities, and a determined and understandable initiative to cut aid budgets. If a program such as this is to approach its potential, it needs to be implemented with a new spirit of commitment and trust.

Our proposals are for strategic purposes that are cost-effective: advocacy of institutional, economic, and political reform; empowerment of people; engagement of citizens as partners for development and in peace-making—are relatively inexpensive compared to other parts of the foreign assistance budget—especially large infrastructure projects. Economies inhere in the activities we are proposing because we concentrate on mobilizing a largely underutilized resource for development: citizens. If commitment to development is limited to small numbers of government officials, foreign donors, and CSOs, then development will never begin to achieve what is possible. Bringing citizens and citizen networks into active play as full partners will greatly increase the resources contributing to international security and sustainable development.

The failure to mobilize citizens as active partners maintains the shadow of dependency, passivity, and fatalism, sapping energy from cultures that need to be active and entrepreneurial. If citizens are a nation's greatest underutilized strategic resource, policymakers should focus on financing initiatives that will empower them to make their full contribution.

Recommendations

To implement the proposals presented here, we make the following recommendations:

1. *Select four or five priority countries to focus on initially and prepare Country Strategic Plans for each.* Focus in the country plans on five or six strategic objectives that would promote significant economic, educational, political, and social change in each country, thus promoting national and international security. We have suggested some priority candidates: economic policy reform, women's empowerment and girls' education, recruiting citizens in promoting democracy and peace, and civil society initiatives in conflict and post-conflict societies. Other potential priorities will undoubtedly arise during preparation of the plans. A final, general priority to strengthen civil society is part of all the others, but it is so important that we also list it as a separate priority on its own.

   The priority in this approach is to develop plans that will

really make a difference, with emphasis on promoting *perceptions* of change with serious communications programs. Defense of the budgets will follow presentation of strategic impacts.[1]

2. *Create a Special Strategic Development Fund that will finance the Country Strategic Plans as well as R&D.* Decisions on funding should give priority to financing the country plans through local or national civil society organizations. Priority should also be given to plans to communicate results of interventions to priority audiences in each country.

    After a few years of experience, the systems developed for direct contracting and grants provision should become institutionalized. Then the Washington-based central unit will be able to focus mainly on sharing information between missions and regional programs to disseminate lessons learned and conduct field support and training programs. Repeating the point made in the introduction, the more independent the funding is, the greater the potential impact.

3. *Create a special fund to promote development of civil society.* The Department of State and USAID should establish either an operational unit—or, better, a semi-autonomous institute similar to the United States Institute of Peace—plus a large central Special Fund for CSO Development. If an operational unit were to be created, it would train agency personnel to lead mission-level programs for collaboration with civil society organizations, provide large "seed grants" for missions to invest in promising civil society organizations, and help revise contracting methods to facilitate new forms of both direct and indirect investment in national

---

1. We are assuming that the total budget produced from aiming at strategic impacts will be "worth it." If not, it will be necessary to modify the proposals, including possibly researching cheaper, alternative strategies.

CSOs. If an institute were established—our preference—it would develop the civil society program, collaborate with USAID, provide large "seed grants" to national CSOs, implement streamlined contracting systems to invest effectively in national CSO strategies, conduct effective monitoring and evaluation activities, and undertake research and policy analysis projects.

4. *Develop a strategy and incentives to transfer knowledge and share lessons of models and strategies that are effective and cost-effective.* Sharing lessons learned is essential to maximize the strategic potential of our proposals. Unfortunately, the non-profit/donor capital markets have weak to nonexistent mechanisms for managing and sharing knowledge across national boundaries. This problem is especially obvious when international assistance is compared to private, profit-making financial markets, which invest massively in knowledge (in developing ideas and products) and finance mass production of products that attract strong buyer interest, making those products available everywhere almost instantly.

In the current nonprofit/donor world, funding is rarely available to transfer knowledge about programs and practices that work to other countries. One of countless examples is an outstanding program done in Peru on the impact of puberty on girls' education. The CSO/contractor produced a product with great potential value in 160 other countries, but not only was there no money to replicate it, there was no money even to communicate the lessons learned. So the lessons lived and died in Peru.

We propose two reforms to correct this problem. First is to include in the funding guidelines of the Special Fund in USAID or in the semi-autonomous institute, an emphasis on financing the cultural adaptation and replication of components of successful reform models in specific strategic areas. This would reward missions and CSOs for replicating effective models.

A second reform would reward the creators of successful models by awarding them special grants as discretionary funding for projects they judge to be priorities. This would provide funding for activities that are crucial for replicating successful models: innovation, research, evaluation, as well as communicating and using knowledge about what works. (If incentives are sufficient, it will be unnecessary to provide for special funding for R&D and communications as called for above. We propose experimenting with both at the beginning and then fine-tuning the combination to optimize between them.)

These proposals, together, would provide incentives for the major actors in financing and producing social initiatives: USAID missions in countries producing innovations, CSO creators of innovations, and CSOs that would adapt and replicate successful model components. We anticipate that most of these programs would be designed by national CSOs to fit local contexts. The objective would be to encourage innovation and entrepreneurship in the social sector. Programs such as these need not involve great amounts of money. Well designed, they should greatly increase the return on investment in social innovations, while also helping encourage the nonprofit/donor world to emphasize entrepreneurship and innovation.

Initiatives with
Short-Term Impact

Although the strategic value of civil society initiatives is often in pursuit of long-term objectives, many current challenges facing foreign policymakers could be mitigated, if not solved, by civil society initiatives that could be implemented very quickly and would show rapid results.

Among the greatest challenges foreign policymakers face today is promoting democracy in countries with a radical, sometimes religious opposition. The threat is most evident in Islamic countries, where people might vote new autocracies to power through the ballot box. Foreign policymakers and international organizations are looking to centrist, secular parties to create real democracies, but these parties are losing power in some places. It is difficult for many countries to help them in part because even the appearance of receiving U.S. or Western help could lead to the use of repressive measures against them.

These situations present a serious dilemma for state action alone, and states have limited options for dealing with them. On the one hand, allied states will avoid contact with groups declared illegal by the other government (the Muslim Brotherhood in Egypt), and they will also avoid contact with groups that have not given up violence (Hamas in Palestine and various Sunni groups in Iraq). Nevertheless, channels of communication are needed with these groups, seeking ways to bring them into the formal political system and also to encourage them to renounce violence. We have shown how such communications helped promote peace in Northern Ireland during the 1990s and helped encourage even paramilitary groups to renounce violence so they could join the formal negotiations that resulted in the 1998 "Good Friday Agreement." Similar kinds of civic engagement played an important role in maintaining the peace in South Africa both before and after the first elections in 1994.

Despite the absence of *formal* channels of communication with these groups, many *informal* channels could be imagined, such as engaging them with CSOs on issues unrelated to the "difficult" issues of democracy and individual rights: economic performance, employment, and the environment. There are good reasons for believing that commitment to civil society initiatives like these could make an important contribution to solving these and other foreign policy dilemmas.

The Challenge
of Social Trust

During World War II, when the country was united behind the war effort, a high degree of social trust and consensus enabled actions and judgments that powerfully supported that effort. Beginning in the late 1960s, however, serious failures in intelligence began to contribute to the ultimate collapse of our policies in Vietnam. One possible reason is that, as social trust declined, intelligence officers skewed their reports, either pitching them to favored political constituencies or—seeking to avoid risks—withholding judgments until they could be read in mainstream commercial media. When social trust is low, policymakers rely on intelligence reports (or bureaucratic decisions on foreign assistance) at their peril. In a highly conflicted political environment devoid of social trust, no reform of agencies gathering information (or awarding foreign assistance contracts) will, by itself, yield reliable judgments—which is to say judgments that are honest and free of political influence, neither slanted to one position nor avoiding controversy.

Bureaucratic risk aversion was widely suspected in the early 1990s, after the fall of the Soviet Union. At the time, the impetus was strong in Washington to spend money in Russia. Almost overnight, hundreds of millions of dollars in "hot money" was dumped on USAID bureaucrats to spend. No one knew how to spend it, so much of it was awarded to the big-eight accounting firms, probably because they were the safest grantees—those least vulnerable to criticism. If the money was going to be wasted—the implicit bureaucratic reasoning must have gone—the safest course was to let the big accounting firms waste it. No one could criticize selecting them to dispose of so much money.

In one important sense, we know the problem of social trust will take care of itself. After 9/11, political conflict in the United States disappeared for a time, and trust was very high; but it did not last. The important issue now is whether we can come together as a people without having to wait for a disaster to make it happen.

It is true that we have focused on issues about which there will be broad agreement. Who disagrees with educating girls or bringing citizens together for peace or economic growth? Yet there are good reasons for believing that the current, conflicted environment, so low in trust, has corrupted and undermined opportunities for bipartisan initiatives. On these issues, however, it is critical to encourage bureaucratic behavior that addresses real problems and provides real judgments about what to do. It is crucial to avoid bureaucratic preoccupation with self-protection, risk-aversion, or judgments heavily influenced by belief about what higher officials want to hear. Our belief and hope is that these proposals will create new spaces for people who disagree on other issues to come together and create trust. To achieve their intended impact, these proposals need to be implemented by people who feel safe to act on their judgment and not feel vulnerable to presenting "unpopular" views. Our proposals depend, therefore, on Democrats and Republicans, conservatives and liberals, coming together and working together to make them happen.

We think there are good reasons why this can happen. These proposals are neither left nor right. Conservatives will support them because they are about entrepreneurship, decentralization, local institutions, and less expensive strategies for promoting democracy and free markets in fragile countries that are national and international security risks. Liberals will like them because they focus on policy reform, poverty reduction, women and girls, the disadvantaged, community revitalization, and non-military strategies for peace. Both sides should celebrate the stronger concept of democratic citizenship, promoting increased public spirit without compulsion. Coming together around these ideas should prepare the ground for significant cooperation, and that, in turn, should promote increasing trust, at least in consideration of these issues.

If we can create new spaces for agreement and trust, we can create new incentives for officials awarding grants and contracts under these proposals to take risks and reward innovations.

Our final thought here has to do with citizens and states. Foreign policy is a responsibility of states. At various times and places in the past, citizens have assumed responsibilities—civil society organizations and even individual volunteers—performing tasks judged priorities by government officials. Now that non-state actors have become the principal threats to both national and international security, we believe that citizens and citizen organizations need to become more important in thinking about the new issues of foreign policy and security facing policymakers and more important in addressing those issues.

Most countries—it is true of countries with both strong and weak democratic institutions—have maintained a strong role for governments combined with a weak concept of citizenship. While this is sometimes not intended (an example is low parental involvement in many U.S. public schools), it is the reality nonetheless. The emergence of global terrorism has created a new reality in relation to national and international security. In a world of increasingly sophisticated and destructive weapons, this new reality needs to bring governments and peoples together as real partners, sharing responsibility for the public good while addressing challenges that are unprecedented in the lives of people everywhere.

Appendix: Outline of Country Strategic Plan for Pakistan

Because cost is so important, we want to provide some estimates of the costs associated with a hypothetical country plan for one country (Pakistan). We want to show that the costs of our proposals are not excessive in relation to the amounts the United States is already spending for programs related to international security—especially other development programs and the military budget. In our hypothetical plan, we are limiting ourselves to the issues we have examined in this essay—issues we chose because we think there would be broad agreement they are strategically important. The task forces responsible for preparing the strategic country plan for Pakistan and for other countries should consider these and possibly other issues. Whereas we can imagine a decision to add one or two additional activities, thus increasing the budget, it should be clear that this broad approach is relatively inexpensive compared to what we are already doing.

These, then, represent a crude estimate of spending for these proposed priorities:

- For economic growth:
  - $15 million for fellowships supporting forty Ph.D.s and forty masters spread over six years;
  - $5 million per year in support for economic policy research. (This program would be greatly strengthened by

creation of an organization like ICEG, preferably head-
quartered in a developing country, that works in all
regions of the world and facilitates south-south networking and learning: at least $10 million per year.)

- Promoting property rights:
  - $20 million over five years ($3 million the first year, $3
    million the second, $4 million the third, and $5 million
    the fourth and fifth). (Part of the funds in the second
    and third years would be available from other interna-
    tional financial institutions.)

- Community mobilization for girls' education, community
  health projects, and (where appropriate) conflict reduction
  and a related communications program: $100–125 million
  per year.

The total for a strategic aid policy for Pakistan, then, would be
in the range of $120–150 million per year. The numbers are not
large for a very large country like Pakistan (population: 160 million) compared to current U.S. assistance to Pakistan and to
military spending in many places.

Contributors

A. Lawrence Chickering is a Research Fellow at the Hoover Institution and is founder and president of Educate Girls Globally (EGG), a CSO that promotes girls' education in developing countries. He co-founded the International Center for Economic Growth and served as its Executive Director until 1998, and he has worked in Pakistan, India, and Egypt. He edited (with Mohammed Salahdine) a book on the informal sector in development, *The Silent Revolution* (1991); and he is the author of a book on American politics, *Beyond Left and Right: Breaking the Political Stalemate* (1993). Chickering is a graduate of the Yale Law School.

Isobel Coleman is Senior Fellow, U.S. foreign policy and director of the Women and U.S. Foreign Policy Program of the Council on Foreign Relations (CFR). At the Council, Coleman is directing a two-year project that examines the effectiveness of U.S. policies toward women in traditional societies in the Middle East and Southwest Asia. Formerly a partner at McKinsey and Co. in New York, she was also a research fellow at the Brookings Institution and an adjunct professor at American University. Coleman holds D.Phil. and M.Phil. degrees in international relations from Oxford University.

P. Edward Haley is Wm. M. Keck Professor of International

Strategic Studies at Claremont-McKenna College. He is a member of the advisory board of the Center for the Study of the Holocaust, Genocide, and Human Rights, and chairman of the International Relations Committee at Claremont-McKenna College. His latest book is *Strategies of Dominance: The Misdirection of U.S. Foreign Policy* (forthcoming, Johns Hopkins University Press and Woodrow Wilson Center Press, April 2006). Haley has a Ph.D. from Johns Hopkins University.

Emily Vargas-Baron directs the Institute for Reconstruction and International Security through Education (The RISE Institute), an international NGO based in Washington, D.C. and Bogotá, Colombia. From 1994 to 2001, she was a Deputy Assistant Administrator at the United States Agency for International Development, where she directed the Center for Human Capacity Development. Previously, she founded and directed the Center for Development, Education, and Nutrition (CEDEN) in Austin, Texas, served as the Andean Region Education Advisor of The Ford Foundation, and was an Education Specialist at UNESCO in Paris. Vargas-Baron holds a Ph.D. in Anthropology from Stanford University.

Index

Abbas, Mahmoud, 71
ABE. *See* Alternative Basic Education
abortion, 51
Afghanistan, 3n2; closed economy of, 20;
  literacy in, 51; local ownership in,
  60–61; nation building in, 62–63;
  society-based initiatives in, 5; strategic
  intervention in, 38, 61; as target
  country, 15; terrorism in, 5, 15, 38,
  58, 60–61; women's rights in, 64
Africa, national CSOs in, 98; society-
  based initiatives in, 5; sub-Saharan,
  16, 49; women's rights in, 49–50, 52,
  56. *See also specific country*
African National Congress (ANC), 83
agricultural productivity, in Colombia,
  103–4; educational gains driven by,
  43, 48–49, 104
AIDS, 95
Albright, Madeleine, 39
alienation, as cause of terrorism, 7–8
Alliance for Progress, 4
Alternative Basic Education (ABE),
  102n5
American Ph.D., 20, 26
Arab world, 117–18; Christians v.
  Muslims, 107; CSOs within, 14;
  disempowerment and humiliation of,
  117–18; families of, 108; girls'
  education in, 60n19; Hindus v.
  Muslims, 74–75; Khansaheb, 40;
  leaders, 93; Muslim Brotherhood, 2,

123; Muslim-majority states, 52;
  progressive v. authoritarian within,
  64; women in, viii, 52–53, 54–55, 56,
  57, 64. *See also* Islam
Arafat, Yasir, 71
Ardito-Barletta, Nicolas, 21
Argentina, formalization in, 36
ASAPROSAR. *See* Program for
  Reintegration and Employment of
  Ex-Combatants
The Asia Foundation (TAF), vii, viii, 5,
  8, 115
Ataturk, Mustafa, reforms for women
  under, 52–53
Australia, national CSOs in, 98

Bangkok, ICEG in, 24
Bangladesh, 3n2; 49–50, 51–52
Barak, Ehud, 72
Barantes, Alphonso, 33
Borlag, Norman, 26
Bourguiba, Habib, role of women under,
  53
brain drain, reducing, 27, 28, 97–98
Brazil, women controlling resources in,
  49–50
Burundi, 86–88, 89–90, 117
Bush, George W., peace initiative of, 71–
  72
Buthelezi, Mangosuthu, 83

Callahan, David, 90